THE AMAZING STORIES OF A BIBLE TRAVELLER

THE CRY OF OUR BROTHERS

**FOR EACH BOOK SOLD A CONTRIBUTION
WILL BE MADE TOWARDS THE PURCHASE
OF BIBLES AND TO HELP PERSECUTED
BROTHERS AROUND THE WORLD**

ISBN 0-9593051-7

Published by:

Rosemary Childs
22 Barncliffe Crescent
Fulwood
Sheffield S10 4DA

Printed by:

ALD
279 Sharrow Vale Road
Sheffield S11 8ZF

OVER 200 MILLION CHRISTIANS EXPERIENCE
PERSECUTION AND SUFFER DISCRIMINATION
BECAUSE OF THEIR FAITH

ACKNOWLEDGEMENTS

I would like to thank Trevor and Carol for their love and support as this book took life.

My grateful thanks to Liz for her guidance and the daunting task of proof reading also Peggy and Carol for final proof reading.

To Denise for her inspiration and enthusiasm.

To Angela and her Writer's Group whose encouragement set this book in motion.

However, the greatest "Thank You" of all goes to my Heavenly Father who, without Him, this book would never have been written.

DEDICATION

This book is dedicated to His Greater Glory

FOREWORD

ISAIAH 6 V8

Then I heard the voice of the Lord saying "Whom shall I send? And who will go for us?". And I said "Here am I. Send me!".

* * *

PROLOGUE

ONE BODY, MANY PARTS

1 CORINTHIANS 12 V12-14, V26

"The body is a unit, though it is made up of many parts; and though all its parts are many, they form one body and we were all given the one Spirit to drink. If one part suffers, every part suffers; if one part is honoured, every part rejoices with it."

THE SUFFERING CHURCH

HEBREWS 13 V3

"Remember those in prison as if you were their fellow prisoners and those who are ill treated as if you yourselves were suffering."

REVELATION 12 V11

"They overcame him by the blood of the Lamb and by the word of their testimony; they did not love their lives so much as to shrink from death."

GOD'S CALL FOR BIBLE TRAVELLERS

JOSHUA 1 V9

"Have I not commanded you? Be strong and courageous. Do not be terrified; do not be discouraged, for the Lord your God will be with you wherever you go."

EPHESIANS 6 V10-11

"Finally be strong in the Lord and in his mighty power. Put on the full armour of God so that you can take your stand against the devil's schemes."

ROMANS 10 V14-15

"How, then, can they call on the one they have not believed in? And how can they believe in the one in whom they have not heard? And how can they hear without someone preaching to them? And how can they preach unless they are sent? As it is written,

HOW BEAUTIFUL ARE THE FEET OF THOSE
WHO BRING GOOD NEWS."

CONTENTS

PAGE NO

x

A COLD DARK MORNING

It was a cold dark morning as we left our hotel. It seemed like the middle of the night. A shiver went through me as we walked down the hotel steps. The six of us were thousands of miles away from our homes, three different nationalities, coming together in a common cause. Each person different in culture, age, background and experience, but all those things were of no consequence. It mattered nothing whether we were married, widowed, single or divorced, whether we were working or retired, whether we had husbands or wives, brothers or sisters. It was all too unimportant for us to even ask each other. All of that was incidental, all these things belonged to our everyday lives to which we would go back and pick up where we left off when our trip was over. But, and there is a big but, I knew that we would all return home a different individual to the one that had left. Our experiences of today would affect our lives like an indelible stamp, which could never be erased. It would be like a birthmark. None of us would ever be able to forget this time we would spend together or this whole experience. We also knew that we would probably never see each other again after our trip was over and we returned to our homes but despite the miles across the globe that separated us, we would always remember each other.

There was also the awesome realisation that, before any of us were born, we had been chosen to be together to be at this place, at this time and in this country - different nationalities from different cultures, to perform together one God-given task, one God-given purpose. However, very soon our designated time would end and we would all go our separate ways. What we had been called to do together, would have been done, God's plan would have been fulfilled - a plan that had been birthed at the foundation of the world. Again I felt the overwhelming privilege of being here.

The cold air of the morning made me catch my breath. The all too familiar back-pack was strapped to my back, the handle of my trolley suitcase resting neatly into the palm of my hand. Their journey with me was nearly over. Soon my precious cargo would be handed over to an unknown brother or sister and their journey would continue, to where, when and how was not for us to know. But that did not matter because we knew that our Lord knew exactly where these precious gifts were going and who would receive a copy of His Word. I mused to myself that one day the Lord would show me what became of these gifts of love but for today we had a task to accomplish, an appointment to keep.

We walked at a steady pace, not rushing. At this hour in the morning to be out and about would in itself draw attention to us. We did not speak; the only sound was the noise of our trolley wheels as they ran over the cracks in the pavement.

After a while we crossed a road and stopped outside a concrete block of flats, grey and ugly in appearance. A Security Officer suddenly appeared from around the side of the building with a gun slung casually over his shoulder. He looked at us with curiosity. "Westerners on their travels, as usual with lots of luggage.", I hoped he was thinking, but then again, I thought, the Chinese people themselves always seem to be on the move and laden down with luggage. He turned and walked round the corner of the building and was eventually out of sight.

We waited in silence, standing quietly as streaks of light started to burst through the dark sky - dawn was coming.

Without hearing them I knew, that like me, my fellow travellers were silently praying, praying that the vehicle we were waiting for would arrive before the dawn did and before the Security Officer returned. It is at these times that you know that you are completely in the hands of God. You can do nothing, nothing, that is, except to pray. I realised then, as I have done in similar situations, that there is no power on earth, no human being, no human resource that can aid you or help you. You are not in control, God is. That is why it did not matter how rich or how poor any of us were, what professions we followed, what contacts we had, how high in society or on the political ladder we were, because none of these things could help us now. We were just six people with a common bond, with one focus and one objective, but it was all in God's hands, not in ours.

Then, from our leader, a whispered, "I think they're coming.". In the distance we could hear the low rumble of an engine, which got progressively louder and then through the gloom we could see a lorry coming down the road driving slowly. Another whisper, "It's them." The lorry came to a halt alongside us; two men leapt from the driver and passenger seats and ran to the rear of the truck. The tailgate was dropped. We each moved forward with our luggage and, oh so quickly, hands helped us to take the packs off our backs and then leant down to pick up the cases as if they were feather-light. There is a sense of urgency about the whole proceedings. Within seconds all the luggage is on board the lorry. I step back from the rear of the vehicle with a weight no longer on my back. My familiar trolley case has gone, disappeared into the blackness of the lorry's interior. Two clicks and the rattle of chains and the tailgate is quickly back in place. Then a hand grabbed my hand and I am looking into a beaming face, seeing a shock of straight jet-black hair, coal-dark almond-shaped eyes smiling into mine. I hear the words "God bless you." and he holds my hand so tightly. A second man appears. Again I hear the words "God bless you." The same shake of the hand in a firm, warm grasp. I respond "God bless you too, brother.". They both raise their hands to us in salute, turn and jump back into the lorry, the engine still running. The lorry is put into gear, the engine revved, the lorry moves forward and picks up speed. The vehicle turns a corner and we watch it disappear. We all continue to stand there in the road. We can still hear the sound of the engine but after a few moments the sound dies.

The early morning silence is with us again. We all turn towards each other. "Well," our leader says "that's it then, lets go home.". For a second I feel emotionally flat and a little bereft. My back feels light, no longer a heavy pack there, my hands are empty, with no case to pull but, oh, then comes the elation, quietly at first and then builds. My heart sings with gratitude to our Heavenly Father. The tension, the pressure of waiting and worrying over the safety of our brothers in collecting the precious cargo, is over. They are safe and our mission is accomplished. Then I suddenly see the Security Officer reappear. He has completed his tour of the building and he looks across at us as we turn to walk away. As before, I wonder what he is thinking. "Strange people these westerners."

I look to the sky and see that dawn is now breaking, the chill is still there in the air, but it looks as if it will be a fine day. Then I hear the whispered words "Let's go and find some breakfast".

THE FIRST AND THE LAST

My fellow travellers will often joke about their positioning as they cross a border in terms of their likelihood of being stopped. You, of course, do not line up behind each other as you approach a border crossing but there is always someone who has to go first and someone who inevitably has to cross over last. Some will say that the first one to cross is more likely to be apprehended, on the basis that you might be the first westerner to cross that day and the guards are alert and fresh. Others say that the last one is most vulnerable because the guards like to get the first flow of crossings underway before they start to select people at random. But of course all Bible travellers know that these assumptions are not based on fact. That is not how it works. Indeed I have been apprehended when I have been both the first and the last and I was last on a particular day, which I now look back on in wonder, joy and gratitude to the Lord.

There were four of us crossing that day, all women - one Welsh, one American and two English. We had returned the previous day from a trip where we had successfully delivered several hundred Bibles and training materials. This was to be my last journey before I returned home. As I was leading the group that day I decided that I would cross last so I could ensure that my fellow travellers were safely across before I crossed.

The bus we were travelling on disgorged its passengers at the border checkpoint. We four were the only westerners on board the bus, the rest were Hong Kong and Chinese people.

As I walked at the back of the column as we passed through the Customs House I prayed for my friends and I knew that they were praying for me.

As the queue snaked its way into the building I saw that one by one each of my friends had been stopped and their suitcases opened on the Customs counter. It's strange because I used to think that if I were apprehended with other fellow travellers that the urge would be to look at each other, to commiserate, (although you are told not to acknowledge each other under these circumstances) but it's amazing, you just don't do that. I watched the three ladies as they stood side by side at the counter with the Customs Officers going through their suitcases. "Well done ladies," I said to myself, "keep up the pretence.". Not one of them looked at each other.

The Customs Officers continued their search. Each case contained a variety of Bibles, training books; hymn books and children's Bibles. The officers were perplexed. Why do westerners carry so many books? One Customs Officer opened a child's Bible but I saw no recognition on his face that he knew that it was a Bible. However the Senior Customs Officer started to become a little agitated. He couldn't understand why so many books were being carried at any one time but he didn't seem to know what action to take.

As I moved forward, I saw how the Chinese and Hong Kong people in the queue were being waved through by the Customs officials. As I brought up the rear I kept walking, following my fellow bus passengers in the hope that they would wave me through too. But no that's not what happened: A Customs Officer called out to me. It was spontaneous on my part in that I looked up at him. He knew I had heard him and seen him. "No escape now." I thought. As I walked towards him he gestured for me to put my black trolley suitcase on the counter as well as my grey nylon bag in which I carried just a few personal possessions. I placed my grey nylon bag first on the counter in the hope that if he found nothing of consequence there then he might be satisfied and not want to see inside the black suitcase. Also as I was the last in the queue and the bus driver was anxious to get us all back on board, as he had a schedule to keep, there was a chance that the Customs Officers would give my bags a cursory glance and let me through. But that was not the way it worked, at least not for me, on that particular day.

I saw the Senior Officer still somewhat agitated about the books that the three women were carrying but he was anxious to get rid of what was obviously becoming a problem to him. Then I saw him nod his head in indication for the cases to be closed and looking at the women he said "Go, Go" and waved his hand at them. "Well Lord," I thought, "I hope that he responds in the same way to me." Besides I was the only one left in the Customs Hall and all the other passengers were making their way back to the bus. The Senior Customs Officer checked my personal grey bag first. There was hardly anything in it other than a newspaper, a water bottle and some sweets. He wasn't particularly interested and he zipped the bag closed, and then he turned his attention to the black suitcase and began to unzip that. He was quite calm now, his original state of agitation gone. "Oh dear." I thought, "If he had been unhappy about the books the others had been carrying, wait until he sees mine," because the only contents of my suitcase were fourteen very large Bibles intended for Pastors. He had managed to just about accept the three previous book-laden cases, but this was too much for him. I waited for what I believed to be the inevitable response from him. I wasn't disappointed. It was too much for him. He lifted out two of the Bibles, one in each hand, his state of agitation having now returned. "This case has just books in it and they are all the same. Why are the books all the same?" he kept asking. Knowing that he couldn't understand the majority of what I was saying I commenced on a monologue about the British being a nation that loved books and that in our libraries we had lots of books that were the same and that was because it enabled lots of people to have access to the same book at the same time, if we didn't do that then there would be long waiting lists of people waiting to borrow the same book and it would take months, even years, before some people would be able to read a specific book. As a consequence we British believed that having lots of copies of the same book was a sensible thing to do. In this vein I waffled on and on. His response was to stand there looking at me asking the same question "Why all the same, why all the same book?". I continued to talk, quite quickly but pleasantly, about British libraries, knowing he did not understand a word I was saying. However I did not want him to think I was being argumentative but I was hoping that if I continued my monologue about British libraries he might become concerned about "losing face" as it was obvious he didn't understand a word I was saying. I hoped then that in final exasperation he would let me go.

He stood looking at me for some moments but I saw something in his face that told me that my appearance with a case full of books, but worse the same book, was the last straw for him. He began to get agitated again and began walking up and down. He had my passport in his hand and he kept opening and closing it. Because of his raised voice and agitated state and the gesticulating of his arms, he drew the attention of the other Customs Officials. What I could not be sure of was whether he knew that the books were Bibles. To this day I still do not know. What I did know, though, was that my chances of getting my Bibles across this border were diminishing by the second. What was adding to his frustration and annoyance was that he seemed at a loss to know how best to deal with the situation he was faced with and that, in my view, created an unpredictable outcome. If he calmed down, I thought, I might be able to salvage some of the Bibles but as his frustration was now turning to anger I might lose everything. He began to discuss the problem with the other Customs Officers. There was a babble of Chinese voices all talking at once with the Senior Official still pacing up and down. Whilst all this was going on, I saw a young Customs Officer, whose age I would put around the late twenties, early thirties, come into the Customs Hall obviously as a result of the fuss and noise being generated by his boss. He was curious to establish the cause of all this disruption. He walked over to me, looked into the suitcase and took out a Bible. As I watched him it was as if, for me, the chatter and noise of his colleagues began to recede into the background and I found myself quite transfixed. There was something about this young man but I didn't know what it was, but there was something. As he opened the Bible I wondered, as I had done about the Senior Official, whether he knew what it was. His face was solemn as he opened the Bible. I watched his features carefully and he started to read and as he did, a smile spread slowly across his face. He laid his hand on the right hand side of the page and he began to stroke the page very tenderly, from right to left. His touch was gentle and he caressed the page as if he were caressing a loved one. For a few moments he was so absorbed that it was as if I and the others were not there.

Then I heard him whisper "Good book, good book.", his voice was barely audible. The Senior Officer had his back to the younger man who had now turned to him and said "This is a good book", but it was as if the words had no sooner fallen from his lips than he seemed to think better of what he had said. He was about to repeat the words and then stopped himself. Very carefully he closed the Bible and returned it to the suitcase and stood back just listening to his Senior Officer, who it seemed had come to a decision.

The older man suddenly turned and seeing the younger officer behind him, he started to issue instructions, the gist of which seemed to be for him to stay with me and my books whilst he went away to seek advice. He then retreated through a door at the far end of the room still clutching my passport. The Customs Hall was suddenly empty, the other Officers having followed the older man out of the room. I looked at the young officer, smiled and said to him "Did I hear you say 'good book?'". He nodded and smiled at me in return. I took out my crucifix, which was on a chain tucked inside my tee shirt. I showed him my cross and said "I am a Christian, are you?". He glanced quickly around the Hall to ensure it was empty and then he smiled again, nodded and said, "Yes, I am". I grabbed his hand and shook it and said "It's good to meet you brother".

Then I said "Oh brother, I must get some of these Bibles across the border, I can't lose them all. How would it be if you looked at the ceiling for a moment and that way you won't see what I am doing and then you can't be held responsible?". He smiled and then he turned his face to the ceiling. I quickly reached into the suitcase and took out a Bible and pushed it into my grey nylon bag that was still lying on the counter. I picked up another and another until there were six of the large Bibles ensconced in the bag. I was too absorbed in what I was doing (as I knew that the older man could return at any moment) to notice that the young officer was now watching my frantic activity. I reached for my seventh Bible when I heard him say, "Please, please, I am a Customs Officer". I looked at him and understood his concern. If I had taken just a couple of Bibles, then that might not create too much of a problem, if I took the majority of them that could make things very difficult for him. "But brother, the bag will only take seven Bibles which is just half of the load of fourteen, it will take no more." However there was no further time for conversation as the door at the end of the room opened and the Senior Officer came back into the room. In a flash I could see the realisation in the young man's face, which was reflected in mine, that the suitcase was half empty now and that fact would be patently obvious to the man who was now approaching the desk. In an instant the young officer slammed down the lid of the suitcase and began pulling the zip around the sides. I, in turn, was frantically trying to zip up the grey nylon bag. I had had no time to pack the Bibles properly and as a consequence the corners of the Bibles were sticking out at various angles through the fragile material. The bag was bulging at the seams. I remember thinking "Lord, he will have to be blind not to see the difference in the shape and the bulges in this bag, which when he left the room was lying almost flat on the counter." I prayed "Oh Lord don't let him notice". I tried to push the bag to my left and I rested my left arm across it hoping to hide some of its bulk and to shield it from his gaze. The senior man spoke to the younger one, obviously giving him instructions. He waved his hand towards me, in a dismissive manner which suggested that I could go, but then his finger pointing to the suitcase indicated that that had to stay. It was all too clear. "She can go but the books are not to go with her." Producing my passport, he handed it to the younger man. With that gesture I was being dismissed. He had solved his problem. A conclusion had been reached by someone, somewhere. The older man was calm now and the incident was over. He turned his back on us and left the room.

The young officer lifted the black suitcase from the counter. I pulled the two handles of the grey bag onto my left arm and, because of its weight, I supported the bag handles with my right hand as well. The young man indicated the door through which the bus passengers and my fellow couriers had departed the Customs House. The driver of the bus had re-entered the building some time ago whilst the Senior Officer had been remonstrating over the number of books I was carrying. He had told me in his broken English that he had a strict timetable to keep and he could not wait for me if I did not get on the bus in the next few minutes. This seemed incongruous to me because whether I got on his bus or not in the next few minutes wasn't left up to me. If it had been, I would be on his bus now! He also told me that I was a bad person for trying to bring all these books into China, pointing his finger at the suitcase. I did wonder, though, whether he was worried that these officials might hold him in some way responsible, after all I was on his bus and he had brought me here. It seemed illogical to me that they would, but I had to remember that my logic was based on the way we did things in England and this wasn't England but China. He had disappeared in a huff, muttering to himself. A few moments later one of my fellow travellers appeared, explaining that the driver was extremely upset and had told them that he would wait for me for a short time and then he was leaving and the three of them had a choice - either to stay on the bus and to continue their journey without me, or to get off. I said that if he decided to leave there was nothing we could do about it, besides it was difficult to assess how long I would be kept here before a decision was reached about what to do about me and my luggage. As I left the Customs House I could not see whether my bus was still parked waiting for me or whether it had departed.

Together the young officer and I walked down a concrete path to a smaller building. Inside there were two Chinese women. He placed the suitcase on the floor and unzipped it. Inside were the seven large Bibles. I thought "If only I could take those seven with me, that would be great." But, oh, I was so grateful for the seven I had concealed in my bag. However, fear gripped my heart when one of the women spotted my grey bag, which I had placed on a chair. "Oh how foolish of me." I thought. "Why didn't I leave it on the floor and stand in front of it instead of having it on full view?". She pointed at the bag and indicated for me to place it next to the suitcase. I said "No, no, it's the contents of the black case that are being confiscated, not the contents of the grey bag.". She still insisted, but once again it was the young Customs Officer who came to my rescue. "No," he said "the grey bag has been cleared through customs; there is no problem with this bag. It is only the contents of the black suitcase which has not been cleared to cross the border". She stood and stared at both of us for what seemed like forever. You could see that she was trying to weigh up the situation, should she believe us or not. "Surely," I thought "she would take the word of a Customs Officer. After all, he should know what goods were to be confiscated and also he was in an authoritative position.". Both he and I stared into that implacable face. Would she believe him, even if she was uncertain about me? Suddenly she turned her back and started to fill out a form in triplicate. I looked at the young man and mouthed a "Thank you." and he smiled back.

13

During the deliberation with the first female, the second had removed the Bibles from the suitcase and it was still on the floor, now empty but with its lid open. Very quickly the young officer picked up the grey nylon bag, dropped it into the suitcase and pulled together the two zips that secured the case. Then, picking it up, he placed it just inside the open door where I could see it but the two women could not. He smiled quickly at me and once again I mouthed a "Thank you.". He then turned to speak to the two women. Finally, and very painstakingly, the receipt was written and a copy handed to me. I moved to the door and took hold of the handle of my suitcase. I walked out into the car park. There were a number of buses parked there, most were full of passengers. I searched for my bus but it had gone. The driver had carried out his threat and left without me. "What now?" I thought. I reached into my pocket and found the slip of paper that bore the name of the hotel that I had to go to, written in both English and Chinese. I looked at the various buses and I wondered which one would take me to the hotel, but for all I knew, none of them went anywhere near the hotel I was seeking.

I turned round looking for help and who should be coming round the corner of the building at the far end of the car park but two men deep in conversation, the Senior Customs Officer and the junior one. I called out to them. Both men looked up. The older man immediately turned his face and walked away, whilst the younger man ran towards me. "What's the matter?" he said. I explained that my bus had gone. He shrugged his shoulders and said "No problem, no problem. Where do you want to go?". I showed him the slip of paper bearing the name of the hotel. "I will get you a taxi." These words had just fallen from his lips when a taxi drove into the car park. "See." he said. "No problem, here is a taxi."

The taxi set down its passenger and the Officer stepped forward. He leant into the car and spoke to the driver in Chinese and in an authorative voice. He pointed his finger several times at the driver whose gaze never left the Officer's face. The driver finally nodded in assent as soon as the Officer had finished speaking. He then turned to me and told me the exact amount to pay the taxi driver, saying "Pay him no more than the amount I have told you. I have also told him to drive as fast as he can to get you to your destination.". I thanked him again.

As I slipped into the back seat of the taxi he placed the suitcase on the seat alongside me. He knelt down by the side door and leant into the back of the car. Taking hold of my hand he said, in a low voice so that the driver could not hear, "Please, please you must come back and bring more Bibles.". I looked into that gentle, smiling face and said "Brother, I promise you that I will come back and bring more Bibles. God bless you brother, for what you have done today.". With that he nodded, stood up and slammed the car door. The taxi turned quickly in the car park and headed with a screech of tyres towards the exit. I knew with certainty that I would get to my destination and that the taxi driver would not cheat me, the young officer had seen to that.

As the taxi reached the exit gate, I turned and looked through the rear window. I did not expect to see him, but he was standing there in the car park, that young Chinese brother dressed in a white uniform and peaked cap and he was waving and continued to wave until my taxi turned the corner and was out of sight. I whispered again "God bless you, brother and thank you Lord, for what you did for me today".

Again I could see that every incident and detail of today's events had been meticulously planned. I had recovered seven of my precious books, not through any efforts of mine whatsoever. I had been like a spectator watching events being played out before me. God had been in complete control of every twist and turn and every intervention by the young Chinese brother. I wondered just how many Customs Officers were Christians and I wondered just how many border crossings there were. The odds on my crossing that specific border, on that particular day, at that precise time, for that Christian Officer to have been on duty and for his sense of curiosity to have empowered him to come forward to examine my suitcase, are overwhelming. I don't believe that any gambler would have made a bet against those odds. I again saw how my Father had planned to the finest detail.

In the back of that taxi I thanked my God for his goodness and his generosity for allowing me to meet so miraculously with that Chinese brother - what an honour!

The taxi reached my hotel destination well ahead of the appointed time. Of course, I did not know whether my fellow travellers were ahead of me or behind. At the hotel I did what I had been instructed to do and then with my seven Bibles still secured safely within my case, I set off for the designated meeting place.

I reached the appointed place of delivery, in a small park, five minutes before the agreed time! "Oh, what a relief." I thought. I positioned my case against a wall and then turned round to view the park and there, just thirty yards away, were my three companions hurrying towards me. It was as if we had never been separated and all that the Lord had done was to take me on a short detour to show me something of His wonderful plan in action and how much He, and not I, was in control. I thanked Him generously for that.

I turned to my three fellow travellers who told me that they had been following me all the way down the road from the hotel, I was too far ahead for them to call out to me and, given our circumstances, they of course knew that it would have been an unwise thing for them to do. I said to them "Ladies, have I got a great story to tell you?". Just then I heard a voice whisper a name in my ear. I turned and there behind me stood a young Chinaman about the same age as the Customs Officer, except he was dressed entirely in black. I told him that we had many lovely gifts for him. He smiled and thanked us. Then he asked if we would pray with him. I was taken back by this because the norm is that as soon as the delivery takes place then our brothers disappear as quickly as they can for their own safety, but here was this young man asking us to pray with him in a very open and public place. As it was at his request, the four of us stood with him and with our eyes open we prayed for him, his safety, for China and all its people. When we'd finished praying he took the hand of each of us, shook it and said "God bless you sister". We blessed him in return. He had a car waiting for him just outside the park and we helped him to put the cargo into the boot. A strong, firm handshake again, from him, accompanied by "God bless you" and then he leapt into the car with the driver moving away before the door had closed. The car disappeared into the melee of traffic and was soon gone from our sight. We turned away, no heavy load now to carry. That same strange feeling came upon me, which I had experienced before in similar circumstances. A feeling of being bereft, my precious cargo was no longer with me, it was with someone else now. But then this was followed on very quickly by the feeling of elation because of the success of our trip. Besides, we were now free to return across the border, to collect more Bibles to take to another brother or sister.

My heart was still with that young man who had risked so much to meet with us in such an open place but then I remembered the other young man at the border-crossing who had also risked so much. I blessed both of them.

The sun was beginning to go down as the four of us left the park. "Come on, ladies." I said. "I know a hotel where we can get a great cup of coffee and where I can tell you about the miraculous things that took place today." "Great." they said, "Let's go". We were no longer hot and tired; there was a lightness in our step as we negotiated the chaos that represents Chinese traffic.

We finally returned to Hong Kong later that night, foot-sore, weary and dishevelled but each of us elated and joyful, what a day!

As for me, I kept my promise to that young man. I did return to China. Nothing would have prevented me from doing so. On that return trip, as the aircraft started its descent into the International Airport at Hong Kong, I did wonder if I might meet that young Customs Officer again. "Perhaps not on this trip," I thought 'but maybe the next one, who knows?". "Only God." I said to myself, out loud.

THE PACK ON MY BACK IS HEAVY

Tired and exhausted, the straps on my backpack cutting into my shoulders through the tee shirt I am wearing, I lean against a pillar in order to take the strain of the backpack and to find shade against the hot midday sun and to catch my breath.

To my left I see the pontoon where our boat will tie up. In half an hour we should be on our way travelling north up the East China Sea for approximately three hours. After that, a bus from the docks to the airport where our flight will take us to the city of Beijing. We had set off at 6 am that morning the four of us, each with our backpack and a trolley suitcase to pull behind us. I look round to see where my three friends are. Each one has found a resting place under cover of the pontoon. They look as tired and worn as I feel. I look at them and feel a sense of love for these three people that I have known for such a short time.

As we wait for the boat, squatting and resting next to our luggage, I see that each woman is lost in her own thoughts. As I lay my arms across my luggage, my own mind wanders back to that weekend when I had attended a conference in England, which focused on the suffering church worldwide. I listened to some amazing things from brothers and sisters from around the world who had suffered persecution, torture and imprisonment for their faith. As I sat there listening, I thought "I know nothing of this". I never knew that in the world today thousands of men and women from different nations are losing their lives because of one conviction that they will not deny and that is their belief in Jesus Christ as the true, living Son of God. "How can this be?" I thought. "For Jesus preached love, peace, compassion and mercy." He wasn't seeking to overthrow governments, to incite riots or insurrection or revolution, except for a revolution in the hearts of men. But he was beaten, tortured and killed, an innocent man sent to his death. "So," I thought "what is so different today?". Jesus is still being beaten, tortured, imprisoned and murdered in the lives of these brothers and sisters who believe in him. Jesus's persecution goes on!

I listened intently to two women who had recently returned from a trip to Cuba. I was interested in hearing about their experiences and the responses of the pastors and Christians in Cuba when they had handed over the Bibles and the other gifts they had brought. What encouraged me was that these two women were ordinary women just like me. As I sat listening to their testimony I kept thinking "I could do that. I'm sure I could. If they can do it, then why can't I?".

I had been greatly moved by the things I had heard. My heart ached within me and I felt the tears close to the surface. 'How,' I thought, 'can I do nothing, having heard the things I've heard today? I can't walk away from this.' So when the Conference finished I told one of the organisers that I was interested in taking God's Word to those who are persecuted for loving Jesus. He gave me the name of the person I needed to speak to and where to find her.

I recalled then meeting Jenny for the first time. She looked up from her desk and smiled and said "Yes dear, how can I help you?". I was drawn by a soft, gentle face with the kindest of eyes. She had a sense of peace and calm about her. I liked her as soon as I laid eyes on her. I recall thinking that here is a very special woman. There was something about her that made her different. "I would like to know more about taking Bibles overseas." I said.

Within me, I could hear this laughing, scornful voice saying "What? You travelling abroad on your own, you must be joking. What can you possibly offer? Who are you to put yourself forward? Arrogance I call it. Look at the size of you, you're five feet and one half inch tall. Oh yes, of course, don't let's forget that half inch that you are so proud of. After all, that half inch will make all the difference won't it? Now then, remind me, what do you weigh? Seven stone four pounds isn't it? Oh yes, I'm sure you have got the strength to carry heavy packs of Bibles on your back and, at the same time, pull an even heavier wheeled suitcase behind you full of Bibles. What a laugh, you can't even steer a supermarket trolley! You've no chance, forget it. We won't even talk about your sense of direction, which I am sure you will agree is non-existent. You can get lost even in your own city. We are talking overseas here, you know, foreign countries where you won't be able to stop every five minutes asking for directions. Well you can, I suppose, but a fat lot of good it will do you, because you won't be able to understand them and they will definitely not understand a single word that you will be saying. If this isn't enough to make you rethink the whole foolish idea, then think on this. Even if you make your application, then can you imagine the reaction of this organisation? No? Then let me tell you. They'll have a good laugh, that's what. 'She must be joking,' they'll say 'but we had better let her down gently. After all, she means well. Her heart is obviously in the right place, but really!' Do you want me to go on? There are a thousand more things I could say but I think you've got the message, haven't you? Therefore, Esther, save yourself a lot of your time and, more importantly, this lovely lady's time and get up now. Tell her you need a little longer to think about it, make your apologies and quietly leave, okay?"

"No!" I thought. "It's not okay. After all, if everything you've said is true, then what have I got to lose? By your analogy, I'm a loser anyway so what does it matter? Sure, I might lose out here as well, so what will I have lost? By your definition nothing, absolutely nothing!"

I looked again into Jenny's lovely, smiling face. "She doesn't look as if she would laugh at me." I thought. "Well here goes."

Some weeks later, I received a call from that same lady with the words "Okay then, where do you want to go?". "Do you mean that my application has been accepted?" I asked. "Yes." came back the response. Wow! I was overjoyed. I asked then if I could go to Cuba. "Yes, why not?" she said and that was the beginning. Cuba came first and then China followed several months later. This was now my fourth trip to China.

As I lean back against the stone pillar, with my hand resting on my backpack on the concrete floor beside me, I think again of that lady and remember all the words of wisdom that she had given me prior to my first trip to Cuba and, following on from that, my trips to China and other countries. "God bless you, Jenny." I whisper to myself. Just then I look up and see the boat we are waiting for coming into the harbour. "The boat's coming ladies." I say. Without hesitation, all three women get to their feet. We adopt the well-practised routine of helping each other to take up our heavy backpacks. Two will lift up one pack between them and hold its weight whilst their companion slips their arms, first right and then left, into the canvas straps. The weight of the pack is still held by the two and is then lifted high on the back of their companion, who then balances the pack and takes on the full weight .The pack is still held until the words "Okay, I've got it." are heard and then the two gently let go. That person will then turn around and with their companion, repeat the same procedure until all packs are in place and as well-balanced as they can be. Each hand then reaches out for their familiar trolley handle to which is strapped the hard canvas suitcase.

For this trip we each have a different coloured suitcase, no black ones, which is great because the black ones can be easily confused with the many black cases being carried by the hundreds of Chinese travellers. Ours do stand out, but what would the security police think? We hope that they will think "Typical of women to have bright coloured luggage. It's to be expected and everyone must, of course, have a different colour. No woman could possibly be seen with the same colour luggage as her travelling companion". We also pray that their logic might be that, if we were trying to conceal anything from their eyes or the eyes of the Customs Officials, we wouldn't be carrying such bright luggage that stands out so obviously in the crowds of people crossing the border. At that moment I pray that oriental logic is the same as that of the west!

"Is everyone okay?" I ask. "We're fine" comes back the response. "Lets go then". They follow me down the pontoon to the boat that is now tied alongside with huge, thick ropes. The boat bobs up and down in the water and then moves to and fro alongside the pontoon, leaving gaps between the side of the boat and the pontoon of between one and two feet. With heavy packs and suitcases that have to be lifted and swung across into the boat, a couple of feet can be extremely hazardous. However, I can see two Chinese sailors standing on the pontoon to assist passengers in stepping onto the side of the boat and one positioned at the bottom of the steps leading down into the boat to take hold of luggage. "Just as well," I think "considering the weight and amount we are carrying.".

As I wait my turn on the pontoon to board the vessel, I wonder about the total number of Bibles we are carrying between us. Because of the distance we are travelling from Hong Kong to Beijing, the time we will be away and the financial cost of the journey, we need to take the maximum number of Bibles to ensure viability of the trip, so that is why our luggage is so heavy. As I walk forward, the pack on my back moves to the right, causing the buckle of the straps to cut into my shoulder and the weight of my load to rub into the bone of my spine. Spontaneously I say "Oh Lord, your Holy Word is so heavy today.". But no sooner have those words left my consciousness, than the stark truth and pure reality hit me, provoking me to say "Oh Lord, forgive me, for I am reminded how you willingly took up and bore an horrendous load, for did you not carry the whole weight of the world on your shoulders?".

Just those few words coming into my mind remind me of all the things that the Lord has done for me and of the great sacrifice he has made. As I board the boat, which would take us up the East China Sea towards our ultimate destination, I am overcome again by the overwhelming privilege of what the four of us are doing. The thought sends a shiver down my spine and once again I am reminded of those words:

"How beautiful are the feet of those who bring Good News."

"Thank you Lord, oh thank you for this wonderful privilege."

I SAW THE FIRE

The lights of the Middle East city sparkled and glowed through the darkness of the night. I felt the cool wind brush my face, but the traditional Muslim black gown and veil I was wearing kept me warm. I could feel the bottom of my gown touching my ankles as the wind blew gently. It was a very dark night and as I stood there on the side of the mountain, looking out over the city, it was as if the whole of the country was laid out before me. It was a lovely panoramic display and I was reminded of the temptation of Jesus by the devil, when he showed him the kingdoms of the world.

As I gazed out over the city, I had the strongest feeling that the Lord was standing at my side and I felt an overwhelming sense of love, a tremendous all-powerful love for all the people of this city - God's love for these His children. It was as if He was showing me and allowing me to feel His love for them, transferring His love to me so I could understand why both I and my fellow traveller were there. "Oh Lord," I whispered "I can feel your love for these people, you love them so much.".

I closed my eyes and prayed silently. Whilst I prayed, I saw darkness, deep and impenetrable but, at the same time, I felt a deep peace. As I continued to pray, I had a sense of a small flame having been lit as if a match had been struck. This tiny flame continued to burn, not terribly bright at first and having little effect on the darkness which surrounded it. Then, little by little, the flame began to glow brighter and to grow bigger as if it was being fed. It was gaining strength by the second. Its glow was beginning to have an effect on the darkness. The darkness no longer seemed impenetrable and through that darkness I could see a city, it was the city I was praying over, the city which lay before me.

The flame, still relatively small, began to glow a bright red and then suddenly it started to descend towards the city. It fell swiftly and surely and as I watched it, flames shot out from its centre point. The flames cascaded into a thousand different directions. They grew bigger and stronger and were like huge tentacles as they spread out across the whole of the city. Then they became as wildfire. The flames were out of control and, within seconds, I saw that the city was ablaze, consumed by the fire. But they were not destroying the buildings. It was as if everything was being cleansed by them, everything rotten and evil was being burnt away. The flames to me represented hope, a new beginning, and I felt that when the flames had done their work, the city would rise up again from the ashes.

To me, that small spark which burst into a flame was God's love, which He had thrown across the city. That love had touched one small part of it, but it took hold, and having taken hold, it became unstoppable and it raged through the city as an all-consuming fire. It could not be controlled. It could not be quenched. No power on earth could stop it. It was on the rampage.

I felt, as I stood and prayed, that this was the beginning. Just one city at first - this city - but then the wildfire would spread throughout the whole country and city after city of this country would be taken by God. These people were His people and they had lived too long in darkness and under oppression. The beginning of their freedom from tyranny had started. I opened my eyes, took in the sight that lay before me, still sparkling and twinkling in the darkness and, turning away, I returned to where my fellow traveller was standing with a young Muslim boy we had befriended on the street one evening. Or, rather, he had befriended us. As I walked towards them I smiled as I remembered how we had encountered him. It had been early evening as my friend (let's call her Steff) and I were walking back to our hotel after having a coffee at another hotel just a short distance from ours.

We had been engrossed in conversation and we were laughing, which we shouldn't have been doing, because it is not the done thing for women to laugh out loud in public and certainly not in the street. We had walked past this young man and his young female friend. We hadn't gone far when we heard him call out to us and ask where we came from. We struck up a conversation with him and his girlfriend and as a consequence we arranged to meet them both for coffee the next day.

This young man became our friend and also our "unofficial" guide around his home city. It was on one of our explorations that he told us that the reason why he called out to us that night was because we had been smiling and laughing and that we had been "so full of joy". He asked us why we were so joyful and what made us so happy. Steff responded by saying that we were full of joy because we knew the love of our Lord Jesus and our happiness stemmed from the fact that we knew the certainty of His love and that His love dwelt within us.

Our young friend (lets call him Hashmell) met with us regularly and Steff spoke more about our Lord, to which he listened intently and asked questions. We had to be careful, for his sake, that his friendship with us did not draw the attention of the religious police, which could create serious problems for him. Whilst I had been praying over the city, Steff had been chatting to Hashmell a little distance away. After I rejoined them, Steff then walked to the edge of the mountain, standing where I had stood, to pray. I then engaged Hashmell in conversation. It would not be in his best interests if he were seen to be standing with a westerner who was thought to be praying. All westerners are assumed to be Christians.

Later that evening, when Steff and I were making our way back to our hotel, we talked about our prayers on the mountainside. We had to be careful about talking openly in our hotel room so we usually conversed quietly whilst we were in the open, ensuring that we could not be overheard. What we discovered during our discussion was absolutely amazing because we both spoke of what we had seen and felt as, individually, we had prayed on that mountainside. We had both experienced the same vision; we had both seen the flame; the same fire; the all-consuming fire, which raged across the city and then spread throughout the whole country, a raging and unstoppable fire. The next day we flew back to England, our mission trip over.

As the months went by and a new year dawned, I began to have this sense of the need to return to that country. However, it was absolutely crucial for me to know that the desire on my heart to undertake a further trip came from God. The desire grew stronger within me as the year progressed. By early summer I felt God's call within me to go back. However, if I were to return, the only time available to me was in early September. I even had the specific dates of when I would be able to go. There was no room at all for me to manoeuvre the dates, they were fixed. It was either those precise dates or none at all.

I prayed about returning to the Middle East and then I telephoned Steff in South Africa. She told me that she, too, had felt the same desire to return but she was seriously inhibited by a very tight work schedule and that there were so few free dates before the end of the year. The only dates she had available would be in early September. The dates she gave me were the exact same dates I was available! We both knew then, for sure, that our trip was in God's Plan. He had called us back. There was no room for further discussion, we were going!

We landed in the capital city of that Middle Eastern country on September 10th 2001, the day before the dreadful happenings in New York, the terrorist attack on The Twin Towers. As a result of this terrible act we were unsure whether we would be able to fly on to the city where the mountain of our vision was located, because the airport in the capital city had been closed. We also wanted to meet again with our friend, Hashmell. Steff had established a lovely friendship with him and we believed that the Lord had his hand on that young man's life. So we trusted God and a few days later we were on a flight bound for our mountain city.

The previous year we had met with no brothers or sisters in that city of the mountain, indeed we had no contact names and no likely locations. However, on this trip Steff had a name and a telephone number. As a consequence, we found ourselves, two days later, sitting cross-legged on mats in a small tea house overlooking a fast-flowing river. Sitting with us was a Pastor.

I am always amazed when I meet men and women who have experienced persecution and who are so in love with Jesus, whether they are Chinese, Cuban or Colombian, that

I am always drawn to their eyes. Their eyes overflow with a special, indescribable love, which shines from within them. Seeing such an outpouring of love in their eyes, I wonder if I am looking into the very eyes of Jesus. This man had those eyes.

He spoke quietly and yet with strength in his voice, which portrayed a total commitment in his love for our Lord. There was also something about him which generated the awareness of the dangers that he knew surrounded him as a follower of Jesus. He knew the risks. He lived, breathed and slept with the knowledge of those risks every day of his life. He accepted them with a gentleness of spirit. There was a feeling of peace that came from deep within him which transferred itself to me as I listened to him speak. This man was special and you could feel the hand of God upon him. He was focused, with his eyes set on Jesus and nothing was going to distract him from his God given purpose.

We asked about his walk with God and his vision for his country. He spoke with a confidence and certainty in his voice. Steff and I listened in amazement when he told us that last year, early one evening, he had gone to a mountain on the outskirts of the city. He had prayed over the city and whilst praying he had seen a flame. A flame which hovered over the city and then burst into life and glowed for a time. Then suddenly, with amazing ferocity, the flame turned into a raging fire and burst forth across the whole city, consuming everything in its path. From the city the fire then rampaged across the whole country. He said he had seen those flames spreading across the land and he knew that God was going to do great things in his homeland.

Steff and I looked at each other in amazement and we asked him for the name of the mountain where he had gone to pray and when he had made that visit. He answered both questions. Unbeknown to him not only was it the same mountain where we had prayed but also his visit had taken place just two days after we had been there. His vision had been our vision. We then told him our story, giving him precise details of our vision on the mountain.

The three of us sat there in that teahouse overlooking the river and all we could do was to smile at each other and to feel a tremendous joy in our hearts. For a while it seemed as if the three of us were cocooned in a private world, bound together by a knowledge to which only we three were privy. Again, as we sat there, I felt again God's love for this country and its people.

Whilst we were with the Pastor we took the opportunity to talk to him about our young friend Hashmell. We told him that we felt the hand of God was upon him, but we were concerned for him because, although he was a qualified engineer, he was finding it difficult to obtain work and he was becoming very depressed. The Pastor asked for his address and telephone number. He told us that he knew the street where Hashmell lived; in fact it wasn't far from his home. We offered to telephone Hashmell to arrange a meeting between the two of them but the Pastor advised against that saying that, in the interests of Hashmell's safety it would be better if he contacted him, rather than us. We, of course, agreed to that. Later, Steff and I prayed that contact with this Pastor would lead Hashmell to our Lord.

We left that country a few days later. I had the strangest of feelings that because of the events of September 11th, a shutter was coming down around that country and that for a while there would be darkness. It was as if, when we left, doors had closed behind us, tight shut, but behind those closed doors there was a man of God who now held a flame, a flaming torch in his hand. The flame had been ignited by God. It could not be extinguished and the raging fire of our three visions will, I know, come to pass.

THE FLAME HAD BEEN BIRTHED!!!

THE PRICE OF A DAUGHTER - 75 DOLLARS

The sun was hot, but inside the hut, with its hard-packed earth floor, there was coolness. This was a hut in a refugee camp. The tiny, painfully thin man standing on my right was a Pastor. He wore a well-worn, battered straw hat, a white vest and light grey trousers. There were well-worn leather sandals on his feet. His flesh was a dark mahogany, his facial skin taut and tight across his cheek bones, with many lines around his eyes, a result of a life spent mainly out of doors, screwed up against the burning sun as he toiled the land. For indeed he had been a farmer, growing maize and sugar beet, before he became a Pastor. He was probably in his early forties, but he looked sixty. Let us call him Francisco. There are many Franciscos in this war-ravaged country of Colombia.

He told us about his small farm in Southern Colombia and how he provided for his family from the crops he grew and from their sale in the local markets. Although the long drawn-out war between the paramilitary and the guerrillas was a constant part of their every-day lives, they remained for many years relatively untouched by it. That is, until one day, a local guerrilla leader paid them a visit. His message to the farmer was short but chillingly clear. He was to no longer grow vegetables on his land; he was to grow plants for the production of drugs. If he refused to do this then his land would be sprayed with a poison that would render the soil useless and incapable of growing or producing vegetation, of any kind, for many years to come. A dreadful dilemma for him, but he could not bring himself to agree to such an undertaking, for in a country whose economy is based on such deadly and evil products and where thousands of farmers grow the plants, he could not in all conscience follow suit, so he refused. His refusal resulted in the guerrillas carrying out their threat - they poisoned his land.

Francisco could no longer provide for his family and no one wanted, understandably, to buy his farm. Why should they? They couldn't even plant drugs in the soil. He faced homelessness and destitution. He could not seek comfort in the knowledge that there would be work for him in the capital city, Bogotá. The city received over 60,000 refugees a day. A city where Government approved teams swept the streets at night and any children found on those streets were shot and killed like vermin, in the same way that they killed the rats that scurried through the back alleys by night. There were too many mouths to feed in Bogotá already, they needed no more to contend with.

Francisco's pain was not to end with the loss of his home and farm; the guerrillas enacted a further revenge upon him. They took by force his eldest daughter. They needed to assuage their anger further, so she became "the prize". Francisco was devastated by this final act of vengeance but he still had his wife and youngest daughter to consider and provide for. He couldn't look to the paramilitary or the police to help, because abductions and kidnappings were everyday occurrences in Colombia. Indeed, murder is common-place, happening on a daily basis with a very low percentage-rate of perpetrators being apprehended. He tried to find work on the land of other farmers but they themselves were finding it difficult enough to provide for their own families. They had their own mouths to feed. After several months with no work, Francisco had no choice other than to travel north to Bogotá and to find a refugee camp where he might find food and some support. However, before he left his farm, his eldest daughter was returned to him. She was in the advanced stages of pregnancy and, therefore, of no further use to the guerrilla leader.

He was now here in this refugee camp where food supplies, although meagre, were available and he could feed his family. There was a small church in the compound and as he became highly regarded and respected by the other refugees they asked him if he would be the Pastor of that church. He agreed and in that church he was seeing destitute people coming to know the Lord. He had paid a high price for this meagre comfort at the camp, but there was no shred of bitterness in this man. I heard no words of anger or recrimination. As I stood in amazement listening to him, I prayed that things might start getting better for him, but just then a small boy ran into the hut, with big brown eyes and a skinny frame and he clung to Francisco's leg. "Your son?" I asked. "No," he replied "this is my grandson. It is the child my daughter bore after her return from the guerrilla camp.". "Where is your daughter now?" I asked. I had half expected her to follow the child into the hut. He hesitated and his eyes filled with tears. He said that the guerrilla leader who had taken her the first time had come to the camp late one night some weeks ago and had taken her from the camp. The message that he left was that he would return her if he paid 75 US dollars for her or, if not, he would only see his daughter again when and if she became pregnant. Francisco gently stroked the head of the young child who still clung tightly to him, a beautiful child born out of rape.

What could one say to a man who had suffered so much? There was a silence and then my fellow traveller asked the Pastor about his wife and if she was here with him in the

35

camp. His face lit up and he smiled as he said "Yes, she is with me, but I am not exactly sure where she is at the moment. She has a tendency to slip quietly away and she wanders the camp. I can never be sure how long she will be gone, but everyone in the camp knows her so I know that she will come to no harm.". These seemed strange words to say. He looked at us and our faces must have reflected our confusion because he then said "Perhaps I should explain. My wife and two daughters were with me on our farm; this was before the guerrillas poisoned the land, when the paramilitary arrived. They said they were patrolling the area because there had been a number of reports of guerrilla activity and they wanted to let the guerrillas know of their presence. The paramilitary left the farm. However, a short time afterwards we heard the sound of gunfire as the military had encountered a small force of guerrillas.

"Fighting broke out and my family and I could hear the battle raging around us. In an attempt to escape, the guerrillas made their way across our farmland and towards the farmhouse. Fearful that we would be caught in the crossfire, we decided to flee but, unfortunately, in doing so, that is exactly what did happen. The paramilitary, fearing that the guerrillas would escape, started to throw hand grenades. As my wife attempted to flee the farmhouse, a grenade exploded close to her. She fell. The guerrillas moved off across the open farmland with the paramilitary in pursuit. I rushed to my wife and cradled her in my arms, believing that she was dead, only to find that she had been rendered unconscious by the explosion and not killed by it. I was overcome by relief, but that relief was short lived because later I discovered that the shock of the explosion had affected her mind. She had lost the ability to speak and the power to communicate. She was left in a permanent trance-like state and, like a child, given to wandering off with no sense of time or place. I have no way of knowing whether it is a temporary condition or whether it is permanent. I pray constantly for her recovery and I do believe that God will heal her."

This man, I felt, was amazing as he had suffered so much and had seen his family devastatingly affected, in different ways, by circumstances not of their making. A lesser man would have been full of bitterness and hatred, seeking revenge against the perpetrators of the crimes against him and his loved ones. He, and they, were innocents caught up in a way of life, in a country full of corruption and evil, with no way out, at least not a way that man could find. However, this man had found the way out, the only way out and that was through the love of our Lord Jesus. The proof was there, standing before me in that hut in that refugee camp, that in the midst of the greatest darkness, when man looks into the deep and bottomless pit of despair, when no human resource on earth can help him, then Jesus will be there. He is the Light and the Way. This man, in his pain and suffering, cried out to the Lord Jesus, the Lord heard him and blessed him. This man came to know a peace and an understanding beyond his comprehension. All feelings of anger, rage and bitterness left him and contentment entered his heart. Love replaced hatred in that man. I saw a peace in his face which was born of the true knowledge that, in this savage and yet beautiful country of Colombia, there was a hope, there was a future, there was a light shining in the darkness, and that hope, that future and that light came from one source, the Lord Jesus. This man knew, with a cast-iron certainty, that all else on earth had failed him, but Jesus would not, and this gave him the strength and courage to face each day with faith and hope for the future, sure in the knowledge that the Lord was with him, loved him and would neither leave him nor forsake him.

He was a blessed man who had been redeemed and saved by the blood of Jesus.

I thought then of my own country, of the faces of so many of my own countrymen and women, so full of worry and concern, despite having an abundance of possessions and with our own homes, cars, schools for our children, food and drink on the table. The Colombian Pastor had none of these things and yet in his poverty he had riches in abundance. He knew what mattered in life, recognising that the materialism of the world got in the way and distracted people from focusing on Jesus. The materialism, the goods and the possessions gave only temporary pleasure, and were soon discarded in a world where there is a lust for the latest gadget or model or state-of-the-art technology. They would all pass away or turn to dust, exposing that the emptiness and yearning within the human soul is still there, having been temporarily camouflaged by the latest possession. Stripped away, there is a yawning chasm but this man, this Pastor was "complete". He was full of the love of the Lord and as I stood there I was reminded of part of that lovely hymn:

> "Let the weak say I am strong,
> Let the poor say I am rich,
> For what the Lord has done for me.".

It was soon time for us to go and we began our farewells to the Pastor. As we were doing so, a woman appeared at the door of the hut. Her looks belied her true age, which was probably late thirties. She was thin to the point of being skeletal, her face was gaunt and drawn, the bones in her shoulders protruded through her skin. Her black hair was long and bedraggled; her dark eyes were enormous in her face. She wore a black and white print frock, which was completely wet through; indeed she was wet from head to toe. I couldn't understand why she was wet because the sun was blazing outside. "Where had she been?" I thought "and what had she been doing?". However, these questions were soon driven from my mind because my attention was drawn and held by the eyes of this woman. Her eyes looked at me but she did not seem to see me or, indeed, register my presence. Her eyes were vacant and uncomprehending. She saw me and yet she did not see me. She continued to stand at the door and made no attempt to move inside. Then I heard the Pastor's voice quietly say "This is my wife.". She looked at me and my companions and, as if in realisation that we were strangers, she blinked and then moved her gaze to a point on the wall and continued to stare at it. But there was something about her which made my heart lurch. There was gentleness and softness and I sensed a loving and caring nature. Indeed, the way in which the Pastor introduced her, his voice low and tender, showed that he had a deep love for this woman.

I walked over to her and put my arms around her. I felt as if I was holding a tiny bird, so fragile that I felt if I hugged her too hard I might break her bones. I felt her respond to me as I held her, returning my embrace. I gently drew her from me and looked into that haunted face and deep within those black, vacant eyes I sensed warmth and a love that was desperately trying to break through. Wherever her mind was I could only pray that it was at peace within her and that the Lord was reaching out to her in the depths of her heart and mind. The heart and mind of man had not been able to penetrate through her deep darkness and reach her, but I knew that HIS heart and HIS mind could. I said goodbye and she smiled at me.

As I walked to the gate of the camp, I felt a great sadness. I had met just one family, in one hut in this camp but each and every hut here would have a family with a story to tell. A story that would be as heart-rending and devastating as the one I had just heard. So much pain and suffering caused by man. But there was a light in that refugee camp. There was a small church, a Pastor and the love of our Lord Jesus Christ. I felt His presence there, I felt His peace there and I felt His love. I saw it in the face of that Colombian Pastor.

As we boarded the bus, one of my companions pressed 75 US dollars into the hand of the Pastor. "For the release of your daughter" she said. He smiled and whispered "God bless you".

VICTORIOUS IN DEFEAT

"I'm not very good at this. In fact, I'm hopeless. What am I doing here, I can't even perform this simple task? All I had to do was to carry this luggage across the border and deliver it. Nothing complicated about that was there?" I asked myself. As I knelt on the floor of the large Customs House, I felt a complete failure. I felt defeated, I felt sick inside. If only I had managed to get just one of these 24 Chinese Bibles across the border that would have been something. I could have felt some satisfaction and achievement if just one Bible had arrived safely. I remembered the words said to me by our mentor back in England. She had said that we had to remember that the holy cargo belonged to God. It was His Holy Word that we were carrying and He was in control, not us. His Word would go wherever He had destined it to go. Even if we were caught at the border and our luggage was confiscated, it had been known for the security police to take a Bible, read it and come to know the Lord. To remember, even at the end of our overall mission trip, that if we only get one Bible through, then that was enough, just one Bible can make a difference. One man or one woman with just one Bible in their hands can take city after city in China for God. One Bible alone can do miraculous things.

Recalling all her words of wisdom, I thought that I had achieved the right state of mind, the right philosophy for dealing with the confiscation of my Bibles or dealing with the issue of being apprehended by the authorities, if that should happen to me but oh boy, was I wrong!!! When it did happen to me I forgot everything I had been told!

41

So what did happen that day that led me to be on my knees at that border crossing?

Well, early that morning I had crossed the border with 24 Chinese Bibles. They were wrapped in clothing in a black canvas bag that I pulled on a trolley. I had been accompanied by a man from Switzerland (let's call him Jacques). We had arrived at the border and stood in different queues. He had crossed the border before me, but as I put my bag on the X-ray machine I saw out of the corner of my eye that he had been apprehended at the Customs desk. I leant forward to take my bag off the X-ray belt and then I heard the high pitch of a male Chinese voice. I knew that he was calling to me. As I lifted the case from the machine I kept my head down, praying that he would think that I had not heard him. What happened next was totally unexpected. The air was shattered by a high-pitched screech of command. The result, a total reflex action on my part, was that I looked up and into the face of the man who had yelled at me. There was nothing I could do but respond. For me to flagrantly ignore him now, when he knew that I had heard him would not be sensible, it would serve no purpose at all other than to aggravate him. It is always important to remember that what you are doing is not just about you. It's about other travellers who will come after you. Your actions and attitude can have repercussions as to how others will be treated by the Security Police and the Customs Officers in the future. You also have to remember that the Customs Officers are only doing their job; they are doing exactly what they have been told to do.

I walked across to the officer and placed my bag on the counter. A female Customs Official came forward and told me to take out the "books". I knew then of course that the

Bibles had shown up on the X-ray machine. There is no way of hiding the Bibles as they pass through the machine. However, it is amazing how sometimes the Customs Officials are, on some days not paying attention, or they turn to talk to their colleagues just as your bag is going past the machine's eye or they are distracted by a disturbance in the Customs Hall. There are times when the machine is out of order or, if the border is extremely busy with large numbers of Hong Kong and Chinese nationals attempting to cross, they don't have the time to carefully scrutinize all the luggage as it passes through the detection machine. However, today was not to be one of those days. There were no crowds at the Customs House. It was almost empty, too many Security Officers with too little to do. I stood alongside Jacques, but we ignored each other. We gave no sign of recognition, for it would not do for the Customs Officers to believe we were fellow travellers, because, who knows, we may in the future have to cross this same border again together.

Having been given the instruction to take out the books, I lifted out just three and placed them on the counter. The female Officer looked at me. "More, more." she said. So I took out three more. I prayed "Oh Lord let her leave me with some Bibles. Don't let her take them all, even if I am left with just one Bible, Lord that will be something.". Then came the order, "Empty, empty!!" I couldn't do it. I pretended that I didn't understand. In frustration, the Security Officer put her hands into the bag and took out all the Bibles, just leaving behind the clothes they were wrapped in. The Bibles were then picked up and taken away. I was called into a side office where I was given a receipt for the Bibles and allowed to go.

I felt sick, I felt a failure. I had this awful feeling of abandon-
ment, leaving my precious gifts behind. My hands were
empty and I felt empty inside. I had crossed the border but
they hadn't. What was the point of that? That
overwhelming love, that promise of eternity, those books of
heavenly grace were not here in this country where they
were needed so badly. "Amazing" I thought "our Father
created this land, and every human being in it, but those
same human beings have banned Him, told Him to stay at
the border, not allowing Him to place His footprint on
Chinese soil.". I had a vision of Jesus. He is standing at
the border crossing, His eyes full of compassion for His
Chinese children, but with wisdom in his expression, born of
the knowledge of what will come to pass in this country of
China. He has known since before the beginning of time.

So there I sat, in defeat, on some stone steps outside a
busy, bustling market. As usual, the place was teeming with
people. That was one of the things I was beginning to get
used to, even after such a short period of time in this
country. There seems to be no peace here with everyone
seeming to live on top of each other and the constant noise
of people and traffic, day and night, which never stops. I
must confess that today I was too absorbed in my own
thoughts of failure, coupled with the constant urge to keep
searching my bag, to notice the noise. I was convinced that
there was one Bible left in the bag. Time and again I rifled
through the clothing. I kept saying "I'm sure there is one
here somewhere". I just couldn't get the thought out of my
mind. However, as my constant searching proved fruitless, I
eventually rationalised that the conviction I had was brought
about because the phrase used by my mentor in England
"Getting just one Bible across the border will make a
difference." was embedded in my thoughts. I looked at the
bag again and couldn't resist the urge to rummage through

it once more, so convinced was I that there was one left in the bag that somehow I kept overlooking.

Finally, frustrated at my failure, I decided to walk through the market to await the return of my Swiss companion who had gone in search of some gypsies that he had met in this city a few days previously. He had brought a pair of trainers and socks with him to give to them as a gift, having noticed that one young man was walking bare-foot. "I will be back in half an hour." he said. He was as dejected as I was, but he was attempting to put on a brave face.

As I walked round the market, my attention was drawn by the yelping of a dog. I drew close to a stall where a man had a number of wire cages stacked on top of each other. The cages contained dogs and puppies, all for sale, not as pets but to be killed, cooked and served up at the dinner table. The dogs were yelping and barking. In a cage on the floor there was one puppy struggling frantically, his paw thrust through the wire, trying to pull towards him a broken saucer with food on it. The tiny dog was yelping and howling in his desperation and frustration. I had been told that the act of putting a saucer of food close to the cage, but yet out of reach of the animal, was a deliberate one. It makes the animal bark, yelp and howl. The noise attracts the attention of passers-by who will then come over to the stall, where they might be persuaded to buy one of the poor creatures.

I went across to the stall and, when the stallholder turned his back, I moved the saucer with my foot, to the front of the cage. Born out of sustained desperation, the animal was quick to seize his opportunity. Within seconds the claws of his paw stabbed at the food. He hauled it into his cage and it was devoured in just one mouthful. The action was repeated once more, with tremendous accuracy. The saucer

45

was empty. The dog was silent, the stallholder turned, his features betraying his awareness that the dog had ceased yelping and crying. His eyes alighted on the empty saucer as I turned and moved slowly away, expecting at any moment to hear the screeching tones that I had come to expect since I arrived in this country, the high pitch of the voice, the shrill, the screech, the gesticulating hands, but I heard nothing.

I continued to walk round the market, my disappointment about the Bibles lying like a dead weight inside of me. I knew that I had to do something. I couldn't return empty handed, so I decided that I would try and collect the confiscated Bibles and take them back across the border with me. The thought of them lying on a concrete floor in a cold dark storeroom was too much to endure. This trip was only my second as a traveller in China. The previous day I had been successful. This was my first experience of being caught and my goods confiscated so it did cross my mind whether attempting to collect the confiscated Bibles was the right thing to do. I tried to remember if I had been told whether this was an acceptable thing to do or not. I could not recall one way or the other.

The rule is that Bible travellers do as they are told, and follow instructions. To start making your own decisions, out of frustration and impatience, can have a detrimental effect not just on yourself and on other travellers who may follow later, but, more importantly, for our Chinese brothers. After all, when our trip is over, we return to our own country but we leave behind many believers who have to survive day by day, not knowing if each day might bring the knock on the door from the PSB, the notorious and brutal security police which would result in being hauled off, men and women alike, to the police station, where they will be beaten and tortured. The strong likelihood of being sent to prison on some trumped up charge of threatening the security of the State and not knowing how long a sentence they will have to serve, occurred only too often.

I thought carefully and prayed silently "Lord, if the desire in my heart to go back and pick up the Bibles comes from you, then I will do your will, but Lord if it is not, then do not 'open the doors' for me. Do not allow me to collect them.". Just then, Jacques returned and I explained my intentions to him. We talked it through and we were both of the same mind. We parted, Jacques going ahead of me. We did not see each other again until much later that night in Hong Kong.

I set off to try and locate where in the Customs House I had to go to recover the Bibles. The Customs building was huge and sprawling, with many floors. Different people gave me different directions. Just when I began to wonder whether doors had been closed to me, I saw a PSB Officer, dressed in his lovat green uniform. One thing was for certain, he would know exactly where I needed to go. As I approached him, I wondered as I have wondered before, where do all the elderly PSB Officers go? I hadn't yet seen an "old" PSB Officer. They were all young, in their 20's and early 30's, all with chiselled features, stoney faced with eyes that never smiled, only narrowed even more so when they looked at you. "Excuse me." I said "Do you know where I can collect these?" holding out the pink, flimsy receipt in my hand. He snatched the paper from me, read it and looked at me. His face was hard and contemptuous. One look from him said it all. I was neither male nor female to him. I wasn't a human being that had rights. I represented to him someone who had committed an offence against the People's Republic of China and, as such, I deserved his contempt. He literally

47

spat the words at me "Upstairs." before thrusting the paper back at me as if it was dirty and he had soiled his fingers by touching it. He immediately turned his back on me, not considering me worthy to be spoken to, indeed his back said it all "It is beneath me to be even seen to acknowledge you, let alone speak to you.".

As I turned away, I felt no anger towards him. My mind held three thoughts, first one of elation. "Great." I thought "I know exactly where to go now." and I felt that the doors had been opened for me to recover my precious Bibles. Secondly, I did not feel hurt or demeaned by his attitude. I actually felt sadness for him, for he had probably never heard about Jesus and how much the Lord loved him. Even if his parents had been Christians, they would have been forbidden by law to talk to him about Jesus and from reading the Bible to him even within the privacy of their own home. Likewise at school, references to Christianity are forbidden; only the doctrine of communism is taught. I could have been born in China; I could be in his position now. If he had never heard of the love of Jesus then how could he be any different? Thirdly, how could I feel affronted or upset by his attitude because for everything bad that has happened to me in my life, I know that Jesus had experienced dreadful things a million times more than I had, when he walked the earth. As he spoke of his Father and of his Father's love, men turned their backs on him, were contemptuous of him, they spat on him, they beat him and tortured him and then in all his innocence they hung him on a cross to die. So who am I to feel offended or affronted by the attitude of one PSB Officer? That was no price to pay.

I finally found the desk where I could retrieve my Bibles. It was on the second floor. A huge room, like an airport lounge but with no chairs, just a few tables scattered around the place. Chinese men leant against the ceiling pillars or perched themselves on the edge of tables, about 20 or so of them in all. They seemed to be waiting for something, or maybe someone, but it wasn't clear to me what they were doing there or what they might be waiting for.

I went to the desk and handed in my pink slip. The female officer disappeared into the back room. She returned with a large polythene bag full of my Bibles and threw them down contemptuously onto the counter. My heart lurched for a second. How could anyone treat the Lord's Word in such a manner? As they fell onto the desk top, I thought of Jesus being pushed and shoved by the Roman soldiers on his way to Calvary and then saw him falling to the ground under the weight of the cross. His book of love was being treated in the same manner, in this age and in this time, in the same way as he was physically abused and treated after his arrest in Gethsemane and on his journey to Golgotha. But again I was reminded of his words as he hung dying on that wooden cross "Father, forgive them, for they know not what they do." and here, today, over two thousand years later, his words are just as relevant in relation to this Chinese official for she did not understand what she was doing.

I handed over the money to pay the fine for the Bibles. She pushed the bag towards me. I thought then how I was paying the price for God's Word with money, but Jesus paid the price with his blood. I made an attempt to offer a Bible to the woman. She raised the palm of her right hand pushing it towards me and, shaking her head violently from side to side, she said "No, no. No, no.". I picked up the polythene bag and whispered to it "Well, at least I'm taking you home with me; I'm not leaving you behind.". I placed the bag carefully on the floor, alongside my black canvas bag and knelt down beside them. I was oh so grateful that the Bibles were back in my possession, but again I felt that overwhelming sense of defeat.

So, I pick up my story again. Here I am, kneeling on the floor of the Customs Hall. I feel in defeat, I feel a failure; I can't even get one Bible across the border. Even the female officer who had returned my Bibles wouldn't accept just one copy. One by one I took out each precious volume and gently placed it back into the black canvas bag. I was so preoccupied thinking that my plans for this border crossing hadn't been fulfilled in the way that I had expected, that I didn't immediately notice the grey polishing mop that had suddenly appeared on the floor in front of me. The strands of the mop were polishing around the canvas bag. I looked up and saw the smiling face of a young Chinese woman, mid to late twenties, I would say. She wore a blue overall with a pocket in front and had small black canvas shoes on her feet. I nodded to her and said "Hello." and before I knew what I was doing I had reached into the bag and taken out a Bible. I opened it and looked up at her. I said "Do you know what this is?". She looked down and began to read, she recognised what it was. Her hand flew to her throat, her mouth opened in amazement and her eyes shone "Oh yes," she said "Bible, a Chinese Bible.". The usual half-opened eyes of the Chinese opened wide in her case and I saw in her eyes and in her face an overwhelming sense of joy, she was ecstatic. "This is for you." I said. She stabbed her finger into her chest and said "For me, for me?". Her manner was incredulous that she was being offered such a gift. The young woman was obviously a Christian.

Then I saw a fear leap into her eyes, she looked quickly to the right and to the left to see if anyone was watching her. She was very frightened, she obviously knew the repercussions of taking a Bible from a foreigner, I also saw something else in her eyes, I saw a hunger. She wanted this Bible and she wanted it badly and I saw that hunger and need overcome her fear. She took the Bible from my hand and within seconds it had disappeared into the pocket of her overall. How amazing I thought, the Bible is a perfect fit, it was as if her pocket had been made for it. There is a bulge in her pocket now but it could be assumed by a bystander to be cleaning materials. I then heard her frantic whisper: "Thank you, thank you". I reached again into the bag and drew out a second Bible and offered it to her. Again, she looked around her at the men leaning and lounging against the walls of the Customs House. Any one of them could be a Security Officer waiting and watching for an incident such as this. For her the second Bible was a bridge too far. "Thank you, but no. No, I have this one" and she gently patted her overall pocket. Again, the quick furtive glance around the room and I sensed that she felt she had stayed with me too long, she felt exposed and vulnerable. "Very well." I said as I replaced the Bible in the canvas bag. I zipped up the bag and then looked up to speak to her, but she had gone. I turned and looked around but she was nowhere to be seen. I couldn't understand why I couldn't even see the back of her in retreat, but there was no sign of her at all. She had left as quickly and as silently as she had arrived. I looked around the room at the still lounging men, no one had moved, not one man was looking at me. It was as if they had not seen or heard anything to do with the encounter I had experienced with that young Chinese woman.

Still on my knees, I spoke to the bulging canvas bag, "Come on," I said "let's go home". In that split second came the revelation, it came to me loud and clear like a cannonball being released from a cannon. It was like a magnificent light being switched on in my brain. Before it had been dark and sombre, now it was as if someone had lit a thousand fireworks in my head. The shooting stars, the catherine wheels, the rockets, the Roman fountains, the sparklers, a truly, truly magnificent Chinese fireworks party, was going on in my head, a revelation indeed. My thoughts were running riot: "Do you not see, child, you are in VICTORY, not in defeat, my will was done this day, my plan was fulfilled, my plan, child, not your plan. The sense you had that there was one Bible to be delivered today was right. I put that thought into your mind and into your heart. All I needed you to do today was to give one Bible to one beloved child of mine. Do you not see how I planned everything that happened to you this day? The words given to you before you came to China were indeed true wisdom, for I have designated each book a precise and specific destination, known only to me. Each and every Bible plays a unique role in the massive tapestry that I have woven before the beginning of time. It is not possible for you to know or understand my every action and my every move. Do not fret and worry again, as you did today. All you have to do is to obey my command and go, I will do the rest. Remember this, child; in doing my will you will always be victorious. How can it be otherwise?".

I leapt to my feet and almost flew back across the border. I wanted to laugh and to cry at the same time and, as ever, I felt this overwhelming sense of privilege of carrying the holy cargo, of bringing the Good News to those who desired His Word above all else.

When I reached my destination, I was ecstatic as I knocked on the door of the apartment. The door opened, my Swiss brother was standing there. He picked me up and swung me round. "We have been concerned for you." he said, as I was long overdue. In the room were two other Bible travellers, an American and a Malaysian pastor. All three had been praying for my safe return.

I told them the full story. In joy, the four of us praised the Lord and thanked him for the wonderful revelation. We also prayed for the young Chinese woman. I was intrigued as to where that one Bible would go. I wondered whether she was a member of an underground church, whether her husband or brother was an itinerant pastor, or whether she had a young son who would read it and would one day take city after city for God in China. I could only wonder but only God knows the answer.

I thanked God that day and that night and I thank Him every time I think of that incident. I learnt so much that day - in fact getting caught, the last thing I wanted to happen, taught me so much. Again, the events showed me that my plans were not God's plans. His mind, his thoughts, his brain are so much greater than mine. Like all mankind, my thoughts, my mind, my brain are miniscule and so non-visionary and I even confine what vision I do have. I do not think big and go beyond and into the impossible, I stay within the possible. I fence myself in and do the same to God. I restrict him to my vision. Oh, how awesome is our God and his works so wonderful and magnificent.

The following morning I went for my briefing for my next border crossing. The Adviser said to me "We have given you the same bag as you had yesterday and we have replaced the Bible you gave away.". He then told me the route to take, which point of the border to cross and at what time. I couldn't believe my ears. "But," I said "that's the same border, the same crossing and at the same time as yesterday!". "Yes" he said in a way that said so? You see, I had understood that even if you successfully delivered a cargo, you would never within 24 hours cross the same border again and at the same time. That's because it's likely that the same border officials will be on duty and recognise you as having crossed the previous day. The Adviser looked at me and said "Yes, I do know where and at what time you crossed yesterday, but I want you to go back and do the same today.". His manner was friendly but such that he was making it perfectly clear as to what he wanted me to do. "Okay." I said. I remembered the advice I had received in England, that I was to do as I was told and to follow instructions to the letter, because those in charge were well informed and highly knowledgeable about what is happening in China and have a wealth of experience. So, do as you are bid.

I arrived at the border crossing and it was amazing, such a contrast to the previous day. Where yesterday the border had been so quiet with hardly any travellers, today there was a mass of humanity trying to cross. The place was crammed with people from both China and Hong Kong. There was the usual sound of raised voices, screeching and yelling. The queues at the desks of the PSB Officers were long. I found it difficult to spot any of my fellow travellers as there were so many people milling about. I looked past the PSB Officers sat at their desks and I could see the familiar counter of the Customs Officials, which faced the X-ray machine. "Are they standing there waiting for me?" I thought. "Are some of them the same as those on duty yesterday and, if so, would they recognise me?'

I then looked down at the familiar canvas bag, which was full of Bibles, standing quietly and peacefully at my side, a treasure of eternity that would set China free. I lovingly rubbed the trolley handle on which the bag rested. Again I realised that this was a true cargo of love, which belonged not to me but to the Lord.

The man in front of me turned and spoke to me. He was a Canadian, who looked to be in his late thirties, and it transpired that he owned a factory in China that manufactured sportswear, specifically sports shoes. He complained about the Chinese bureaucracy. He said they were good workers but the amount of time he had to spend in completing the various kinds of paperwork was burdensome in terms of time and money. At one point he opened his bag to show me examples of the sports shoes his company made. I was so preoccupied with our conversation that, before I knew it, he was at the front of the queue and then with a farewell and a wave of his hand he moved across the red painted line to stand in front of the PSB Officer's desk. Then with passport in hand he turned, gave me a final wave and moved towards the X-ray machine.

I then moved across the red line, handing my passport to the PSB Officer, not once looking at his face and when I had to look at him, I avoided his eyes, concentrating on his mouth. Soon there was the familiar throw of the passport onto the side of the desk, the dismissive air given to a westerner, an imperialist. I grinned to myself. "He can think what he likes of me." I thought. I am past him now and it's just the X-ray machine and the Customs Officers to contend with.

However, as I walked towards the X-ray machine, I decided that I would not put my bag onto the belt. I would walk past the long cumbersome tunnel-like equipment and I would pray that no one would notice me. So that is what I attempted to do. But someone did notice me - a little plump, middle-aged Hong Kong lady who had just placed her bags on to the X-ray machine's conveyor belt. She thought she was being helpful in assisting a foreigner who obviously didn't know how things were done! With a smile on her face she gestured to me that I had to put my bag on to the conveyor belt. I smiled back at her pretending that I didn't understand. "Bag to go on there." she said, pointing to the black belt again. "Yes, yes." I said, trying to look as if I was a first-time traveller, a novice who did not understand the ropes, whilst all the time praying that her actions would not draw the attention of the Customs Officers to herself and then to me. "Oh please go away." I thought. "I know you mean well but please stop trying to be helpful, at least not to me and not today." I nodded to her and grinned again and continued walking. Then, thankfully, I saw her smile fade and I could see that she had resigned herself to the fact that this westerner was not going to understand her. So, with a shrug of her shoulders, she turned away and concentrated on recovering her luggage which the X-ray machine was now disgorging.

I kept walking slowly, not hurrying. At every step I expected to hear a high pitched yell from the Customs desk, for even if they had not seen me avoid the X-ray machine, they could still pick and choose whoever they felt inclined to stop. I could see the long counter to my left, beyond that was a wall and I knew that once I reached that wall I would be out of their line of vision. I quickly glanced sideways and saw a large number of Chinese people gathered in front of the Customs desk, two persons deep in some places. All were talking, gesticulating and generally adding to the melee of noise and chaos. I caught just a quick glimpse of the cap badges of the Customs Officers. My heart was pounding like a drum; my every footstep seemed to be in time to the pounding of my heart, so loud was it that I thought everyone around me would hear it. In my mind I kept hearing the words "Don't rush, walk slowly, don't draw attention to yourself.". Every fibre of my body was urging me to run. But it was as if there was a hand on my right shoulder which was dictating the pace and rhythm of my steps. Deep down, I felt that even if I tried to run I wouldn't be able to, someone was in control of my every movement. Suddenly, there was the wall, six, five, four more steps and I would reach it and then, wonderfully I was alongside it out of view of the Customs Officers.

I walked towards the escalator which would take me down to the ground floor and to the exit of the building. "Don't increase your pace." I said to myself. "You are not safe yet, you can still be brought back." In that building there are police who are watching and scanning the travellers looking for anyone who looks suspicious, or is behaving in a way that arouses their curiosity. Then, suddenly, I was outside the building, savouring the fresh air. I had this tremendous urge to jump up and down and yell and to let out all the exuberance inside me, which was welling up like a bottle of champagne that had been shaken, to pop its cork and to flow from me. However, I disciplined myself to stay calm. I looked around and saw my fellow traveller waiting for me at a slight distance. We nodded to each other. We had both got through with our holy cargo intact. He smiled and I could see the same exhilaration on his face. We didn't need to speak, there was no need for words, our smiles said it all. We safely delivered our precious cargo to the very place where I should have gone the previous day, but, of course, on that day, God had a much bigger and better idea. Our delivery done, my fellow traveller and I returned to Hong Kong, crossing a different border, to the one we had used that morning.

On the return journey I thanked the Lord. The 24 Bibles were now where God had destined them to be - the 23 Bibles I had carried yesterday, plus the replacement one. Again, that day I had seen His work and His plan in action. Within 24 hours I had crossed the same border, at the same time with the same Bibles, but the events had been so very different. The teeming crowds, the chaos, God had planned all that. It was as if He was telling me again "Do you now see, child, why you should not worry? Yesterday there was a specific job for you to do and today a different one, but both fulfilled my PURPOSE at the RIGHT time and at the RIGHT place according to My Plan. So, therefore, remember, it does not matter what border you cross, at what time and at what place, for I will be with you. I am in control, it is my battle and you are completely in my hands, remember that.".

Upon my return home to England, there was a further revelation for me. I spoke to my English mentor about the young Chinese woman I had met and she said "Do not fail to appreciate the wondrous works God has done on your trip. Think about this carefully, God took one English woman from one side of the world to the other, to meet with one Chinese woman at a set date, at a set time and at a set place and to give her one Chinese Bible. A perfect plan, timed to the ultimate second. The meeting was over within minutes but God's plan was fulfilled, a plan that was designed long before either of you were born!".

MONEY FOR FOOD

I tore open the envelope and pulled out a card. As I looked at the lovely picture of wild flowers on the front, something slipped from inside and fluttered to the floor. I picked it up and turned the paper over. It was a cheque for forty pounds. I looked at the card again, intrigued to see who the cheque had come from and what it was for. Looking at the name at the bottom of the card, I was delighted to see that it was from a lovely Welsh woman that I had met in China during my last Bible trip. My mind went back to that trip and I remembered how she had carried very heavy packs of Bibles on her back despite her suffering from an arthritic condition. There had been times when I had seen her face etched in pain but she had never complained, not once. I had admired her endurance and her determination.

There was something else that I knew about her, that she was a widow and lived alone in a remote location in Wales. Financially the Bible trip to China had been a struggle for her and, from things she had said during our travels together, I had concluded that there was very little money to spare. Therefore I was taken aback when I received this cheque from her for forty pounds. I sat down and picked up the card from which the cheque had fallen and started to read.

I won't call her by her real name, but I will give her that lovely Welsh name of Bronwyn. In her letter Bronwyn spoke of my forthcoming trip to the Middle East. She said that she would have liked to have come with me but, as that was not possible, she promised that each day whilst I was away she would pray for me. She had been praying for the Christians in that country and the cheque she had placed in the card was to be used to help them. The words she used were "This is money for food for Christians in that country who are poor and in desperate need.".

"Money for food" were the words I repeated when, two evenings later, I was with my fellow traveller and our mentor preparing for our flight the next morning. When the mentor read the message from Bronwyn and saw the cheque, she said "She can't afford that, that's an awful lot of money for her to give.". When I asked what we should do with the money, "Respect her wishes." came back the reply.

My fellow traveller who had sat quietly and said nothing during the conversation suddenly said "How very strange.". She then related how before she had left her home in South Africa an American friend had sent her money and had asked that she use it wherever she felt it was most appropriate, during her trip. She counted out the money and it was just under 1,000 US dollars. "How wonderful," we thought "that we should receive two gifts of money from two different sources to be used for God's work.".

It was suggested that it would be sensible to convert Bronwyn's money into US dollars and put the two amounts together. This we did and it was amazing because the total amount came to exactly 1,000 dollars. What was also truly amazing was the fact that that the two individuals had given the maximum of what they could afford. The American donation came from someone who could afford to give more than Bronwyn but nevertheless had given just what he was able to give and Bronwyn had done exactly the same. The amounts they had given individually were immaterial. I believe that God had honoured the giving of both and this was demonstrated in the way in which the two separate sums of money when combined made the exact sum of 1,000 dollars. Thinking of Bronwyn, I was also reminded of the widow's mite. When Jesus saw the rich putting their gifts into the temple treasury, he also saw a poor widow put in two very small copper coins and he said "I tell you the truth, this poor widow has put in more than all the others. All these people gave their gifts out of their wealth; but she out of her poverty put in all she had to live on".

Armed with such a sum of money we felt apprehensive and concerned. After all, we met so few people on our visits to that Middle East country and those that we did meet, our time with them was so short that trying to determine whether there was a financial need was almost impossible. "Therefore," we asked ourselves "how would we be able to decide where best to give the money?". Bronwyn's words came back to me again, "This is 'money for food'.". "But how" I thought "will we be able to meet with those who needed money to buy food, how would we find them?". Previous trips had not allowed for this kind of encounter to take place. I was somewhat perplexed but, of course, there was the obvious answer. Our mentor said "Let us pray about it, let's ask God for wisdom and guidance.". The three of us that evening prayed that God would guide us in ensuring that the money would go where God had planned for it to go.

Two evenings later my fellow traveller and I were several thousands of miles away from England, in our hotel room. It was around 7.30 pm. We donned our black gowns and pulled on the black veils that completely covered our heads and necks. We then picked up our large plastic bags which contained the precious gifts of love. We glanced at the clock, it was time. We slipped quietly from the hotel,

61

walking slowly with heads suitably bowed in the style of the women of that country.

The night was dark and chill as we turned from the hotel into the street. The air was still full of dust and grime. The traffic of this city polluted the atmosphere to the point where my throat seemed to be constantly full of grit. The cacophony of traffic noise and car horns, which were incessant during the day, had now died down.

I found no charm in this city where the pavements were punishing to the soles of your feet. There was no warmth, no atmosphere of joy or pleasure. Walking round the city streets, where shops were in abundance, one expected to feel some warmth, a convivial atmosphere amongst the people that walked the streets and went about their day to day business, or indulged in some shopping, but there was nothing like that. It seemed as if something was missing. The air was not charged with the kind of hustle and bustle that I am used to at home, although I did not expect it to be like a city in my own country, neither did it reflect any other cities that I had been to in numerous countries around the world. There was an oppressive air, a feeling of being stifled, of rigid conformity. This was of course reinforced by the mass of black-gowned women that one passed on the streets going about their daily routine. Young and old alike, they were enveloped from top to toe in black - sombre, death-like and yet, many of the young women were quick to smile. If you smiled at them they would at first look very startled but then, like the reaction of the majority of human beings, they couldn't help themselves in returning the smile. The older women were not so forthcoming and, of course, you would never, ever smile at a man in this country - that is totally unacceptable.

I sensed that here was a country where many of its people were tired of the yoke they laboured under, here was a people ready to break free from their oppression. There was a sense of a thirst for freedom in the air. I felt it was just a question of the right time and the right moment - God's right time and God's right moment.

All these thoughts went through my mind as we waited at the designated place. The night was chill and the streets were nearly deserted, although by western standards it was still early evening. We needed to be careful because it was unusual for women to be seen out on the streets after dark and we did not wish to draw attention to ourselves. We waited patiently in the darkness, occasionally strolling back and forth along the pavement not wanting to be seen standing in the same place for any length of time.

As the chillness of the night increased then so did the chill in my heart. My companion and I exchanged worried glances as we waited anxiously to meet our brothers who should have by now arrived to collect these precious gifts. I could see from her expression that she was experiencing the self-same thoughts that I was having. "Where were they? What had happened to them? Why weren't they here? Was it too dangerous for them to meet with us tonight?" But the thought that was uppermost in our minds was "Were they safe?" We prayed silently that no harm had befallen them. The night drew on and the chill air crept into our bones. We continued to wait but, finally, we had to accept that no one was coming to meet with us. Reluctantly, we nodded to each other and with shoulders bowed we turned together to walk back to the hotel. We prayed that when we returned to our room there might be a message of some kind from our friends to say that they had been unable to meet with us this evening, that they would see us tomorrow night. However, there was no such message waiting for us.

The two of us sat in our room and prayed silently. We felt disappointed because we had so looked forward to this evening when, for just a few brief moments, we would have met with some unknown brothers and handed over to them the most precious gifts that they were desperate to receive - but it was not to be.

However, we did have a fall-back position. We had been given a name and an address to go to if our meeting did not take place as planned. We had been told this person would help us and so, the next day, we decided to seek him out. The following afternoon saw us standing before a wrought-iron gate. It had taken us some time to find the right location. Having rung the bell attached to a high stone wall, we peered through the iron gate. There was silence. No sound of any kind to give an indication that anyone was at home. We waited and silently prayed. We pressed the bell again and then we heard the noise of a door closing, followed by footsteps. Round the corner of the building came a man, obviously in a hurry, and he was striding quickly down the path towards us. He seemed very preoccupied. Indeed, there was a look of surprise on his face as he saw the two of us peering at him through the iron gate. We could not be sure that he had heard the ringing of the bell, or indeed, whether this was the man we were seeking. After all, it was a large building and many people may be in residence there for all we knew.

He opened the gate and made to pass through. He hesitated and looked at us for a moment and my companion told him the name of the man we were seeking. He hesitated for a second, looked at us both as if trying to assess what two western women might want with this man and then he said somewhat cautiously "I am he". We smiled at him and said that we needed to talk with him. He still seemed very wary of us and, as my companion opened her mouth to speak again to explain the circumstances that had brought us to his door, he quickly intervened saying "I am very late for a meeting. My car is just round the corner, come with me and we will talk in the car". He turned and walked very quickly towards a car that was parked at the end of the road. We followed almost at a running pace in order to keep up.

As we approached the car, my companion and I looked at each other, glad that we had located the man we were seeking. But he didn't seem very forthcoming, indeed it was as if he did not like being seen with us. We had been as cautious as we could be and had kept our voices low when we had spoken to him and we were trying our utmost to be discreet. But, as we hurried after him, the thought going through both our minds was "Would he be able to help us?" or, indeed, "Would he want to help us?". We were not sure as, so far, his manner had not been terribly welcoming.

Having reached the car, he opened the rear door and stepped back to allow the two of us to scramble into the back seat. He closed the door, slid into the front seat and started the engine. As he looked over his left shoulder to check for traffic, he asked which hotel we were staying at and we told him. "Okay" he said "I will drop you off close to your hotel on the way to my meeting". Then as he moved the car out into the traffic he turned and smiled at us. The atmosphere changed completely "I am so sorry" he said. "I have to be very careful. Now that we are in the car it is safe for us to talk." His face took on a whole new countenance;

he grinned at us and welcomed us to his country. He confirmed that he was the Pastor we were seeking.

We then spoke of the friends that we had in common back in England and he smiled and laughed as he recalled his meetings with them when they had visited him the previous year. He asked us to pass on his blessings to them when we returned home.

He, of course, knew why we had come to his country and he also understood the circumstances had led us to seek him out.

We then explained to him what had happened the previous night, or rather what did not happen. He nodded and said "Do not worry, leave it to me. This evening just go to the same place at the same time as you did last night and wait.". We thanked him and he in turn blessed us for coming.

We knew nothing about this Pastor and indeed why should we, other than to know the part he would play if our meeting did not take place as planned. We had assumed that he and his flock would be recipients of the Bibles we had brought. So he amazed us when he said "In what language are the Bibles that you have brought here?". Having told him, he responded with "Oh, I see.". We were curious as to his response and said "But is that not your language?". He replied "Yes, but my congregation worship in a different language in line with their ancestral and cultural background. We need Bibles in our own language.".

So here was a man who was putting himself at risk in order to get Bibles to another Pastor and his congregation. Neither he, nor his flock would benefit from what we had brought. We then asked him what were his needs, and those of his congregation. He said "We need Bibles in their mother tongue". We told him that we would tell our friends when we returned home to see what they could do to help. He thanked us. We also asked him about his congregation and the smile left his face, his voice became serious as he said "My congregation is growing, praise the Lord for that, but with the increase come more and more widows with children and they are in such great need. I have so many widows now and there are so many children that need to be fed. Feeding these women and children is becoming, daily, an enormous problem for me. What we desperately need for these widows is money for food".

Those three words "money for food" were said so quietly by the Pastor but, to the two of us, it was as if he had shouted them. My companion and I looked at each other and smiled. So this was it. Bronwyn's very words, "money for food". The Pastor continued to talk about his widows and their children whilst the two of us nodded together in assent. My companion put her hand into the pocket of her black gown and took out the 1,000 dollars and held it in her hand. The Pastor steered the car across the traffic in order to drive towards our hotel which we could now see in the distance. My companion said very quietly "Pastor, here is the money for food, for your widows and their children.". At her words he turned to look at her and in that moment she placed the money in his hand. He didn't know what to say. He was completely speechless. He steered the car towards the pavement outside our hotel. His face was an amazing sight to behold. He turned to bless us, but we said the blessings belonged not to us but to a Welsh lady who was a widow herself and to a gentleman in America.

We got out of the car and waved him goodbye. We waited by the side of the road long after his vehicle had disappeared into the traffic. After all, we had a thousand joyous thoughts running riot through our minds. We asked ourselves whether it was for real, in terms of the events that we had just experienced. Did it really take place? What seemed like a long period of time since arriving at the Pastor's gate to now finding ourselves back outside our hotel, was in fact only a matter of fifteen to twenty minutes. Such a lot had taken place during that short period of time.

We were both full of such joy that we felt we could have burst. It was miraculous and we praised the Lord for what he had done that day. We were so amazed to realise that the very words used by one widow who lived thousands of miles away from this country should have been repeated by that Pastor and that her "money for food" would now benefit widows and their children in this country. Bronwyn had said to me before I left England that it was not possible for her to come to this country with me, she was wrong. She did come with me and was a tremendous blessing, as a widow herself, to so many other widows that she will never meet, at least not this side of heaven.

The story does not end there, though. On the contrary, as always, with our gracious Lord it gets better and better. That same evening we were about to leave our hotel for our appointed destination when the telephone rang. Picking up the phone I recognised the voice of the Pastor who had been with us earlier in the day. He said "All is well and going to plan. I had hoped to see you this evening but, unfortunately, I will be unable to come. I wanted to say goodbye to you both personally, to bless you again for coming and to ask you to thank the two people that provided

68

that wonderful gift". I told him that we would pass on his blessings to them.

That evening, with heavy bags, we left the hotel for our appointed destination. In the darkness we waited quietly and silently. The self-same questions were going through our minds as they did the previous evening. "Would they come? How many brothers would there be? Was it safe for them to come tonight?". As these thoughts ran through our minds, we saw a young man turn the corner and walk towards us. It was difficult not to raise our hopes with questions such as "Is this the one we are waiting for?" And, just when you think it might be, he walks past us. Your pounding heart returns to a normal beat until, once again, you hear a noise and recognise footsteps making their way towards you and the pounding of your heart starts all over again.

However, that night we did not have to wait very long. Two brothers did arrive and we handed over our precious gifts to them. Everything went perfectly to plan. We quickly said our farewells to them and I have a wonderful lasting memory of two young men with very dark eyes shadowed by thick, black eyebrows, olive-skinned and with smiles on their faces that said it all. There was no need for words. Just time in a fleeting moment to grasp the hands of our two brothers in Christ, for them to murmur a warm, heartfelt "God bless you." and then for them to wave as they quickly drove away to be soon lost in the darkness. The waiting was over. God had done His work. We turned out of the dark, ill-lit street and walked back to our hotel.

Then of course comes the time for reflection and to marvel at the things God had done. "Isn't it amazing?" we thought as we looked back over the last twenty four hours at the things that had happened and what had taken place in that relatively short space of time. Only last evening we had been worried and concerned about our inability to meet with our brothers, coupled with a sense of disappointment that the meeting had not taken place as planned. But, of course, now we knew that that had been our plan, not God's plan. If those two young men had turned up last night, as arranged, then we would not have gone searching for our Pastor, the Pastor that God had wanted us to find so that we could give him that precious gift of money for his widows and their children. Under normal circumstances it would not have been possible to meet this Pastor. The only means of meeting him was if our plan went wrong. And, of course, that is exactly what did happen and now, here we were, our original plan back on schedule, having now met our two brothers and handed our Bibles safely over to them.

We never did discover the reason as to why the meeting did not take place on that first evening. But of course, having said that, one knows immediately why that meeting did not take place. It taught us so clearly that God's plans are not our plans, His timing is not our timing. All we have to do is to be obedient to God, leave everything in His hands and trust that He will do the rest.

It's as simple as that!

WHAT AM I DOING HERE?

What am I doing here? That's the question I was asking myself as I stood on a platform in a church located in a small village in Colombia with over 700 Colombian Christians gazing up at me. The structure of the church could best be described as barn-like with the doors at the rear, open to the morning sunlight. The blue Colombian sky was bearing the promise of a lovely warm day even though it was the month of November.

I looked about me. The Pastor of the church, let's call him Eduardo, was sitting on the front row with one of my two fellow travellers occupying the seat next to him. They were both smiling up at me, giving me encouragement. Standing alongside me on the platform was my other travelling companion Reynard, a true giant of a man in every sense of the word. He was German and stood tall at 6 foot 6 inches. He had been a Pastor for many years in Ecuador, a fascinating man who was a powerful man of God. He turned to me and smiled. I then noticed many of the congregation smiling as I stood next to Reynard. The irony of the situation was not lost on either of us, as we realised what an amusing sight we portrayed. Reynard was looking even taller than his normal six and a half feet because the platform on which we were standing gave him another three feet in height and I was stood beside him, all of five foot (and the half inch!).

Reynard and I smiled back at them in realisation of the picture we presented. But, oh, how marvellous was the further realisation of what God was saying. Our

71

circumstances showed so clearly to them and to us, how God uses everyone. Here we were, the two of us, so opposite in every way - our nationalities, our ages, our backgrounds, our speech, our height, our physical builds, our lifestyles. After all, here was a shy, introvert woman, standing alongside an extrovert, exuberant man, an experienced Pastor. On the face of it, the world would say "What have these two got in common? Absolutely nothing - you couldn't find two more opposites if you tried. Who decided to let these two come together on this trip? They obviously did not consider what kind of picture they would make standing side by side. Their credibility will be shot to pieces. Well I suppose they will provide a source of amusement if nothing else". Now that is man's perception but certainly not God's.

In those first few moments of standing on the platform at the front of that church, as yet with no words spoken by Reynard or myself, I realised that words were totally unnecessary. What we two represented, standing there in silence, spoke thunderous volumes. Just our presence together said it all. The world saw us one way but God saw us another. He was saying so very clearly "Look at these two and see how different they are and yet I use both of them for the glory of my Kingdom. All my children are different; every child of mine is unique because I made you all that way. There are no duplicates and every child is special in my eyes. These two children have their strengths and they have their weaknesses but I take their strengths and strengthen them further. I take their weaknesses and turn them into strengths. I look not at what is on the outside but what is on the inside. I see their hearts. There are no exceptions for me. I love all my children and I delight in their differences". I knew then, in that moment, what I was doing there. I realised that I did not need to be a great orator, or to deliver a sermon like Billy Graham, or to preach the way that Reynard did. All I had to do was to listen to God's call to go to Colombia and to be just me and in doing so He would do the rest.

As I stood before that large congregation, thousands of miles from home, I felt a tremendous peace and tranquillity descend upon my heart. I knew then with absolute certainty that I was meant to be there.

As I again looked at these Colombian Christians, I wondered what I could possibly say to these people whose faces were so full of the love of our Lord. I knew nothing of persecution, nothing of fear, the cold, clammy, terrifying fear of being awakened during the night by a loud banging on my door which would signify my arrest, imprisonment and possibly my death, so what could I say to them? I had nothing to give to them, if anything they had a lot to give me and to teach me.

These dear people gave me cause to search my soul and to see my poorness in relation to their richness. The world I come from is so rich in materialism that in comparison they are so poor. But our materialism is our greatest enemy because it gets in the way of our relationship with God. We all know, in western society, that whatever we seek to possess, whether it be a bigger house, or a new car or the latest hi-tech computer, that once we have acquired it, after a short time that possession ceases to satisfy us and we look to possess the next thing on the market. We chase after the latest product, whose marketing language promises that this is the thing that will satisfy all our needs. This is the product which will fulfil all our dreams and we need to look no further. This is the answer!

However, although we want to believe that we have found what we are truly seeking, we know deep in our hearts that once we possess it, it will only satisfy us for a short while. It is like a dance that is continuous. Whilst we are dancing we feel exhilarated but then, after a short while, the music ends and that dance is over. The exhilaration is gone. We come back to reality and feel an emptiness. We want to feel good again so we call for more music and another dance and the process starts all over again and so it goes on. The dance becomes continuous in our frantic search for satisfaction and to fill the ever-aching void in our hearts. If we never get off the dance floor and do not admit the truth, that materialism will never supply our deepest need, and do not start to seek true fulfilment, then the dance will go on throughout our lives and become our dance of death. We will never have seen the truth. I believe that within each and every one of us there is this urge, this uncontrollable need to fill the emptiness inside us. We hunger and thirst for this void to be filled. That emptiness, that void, can only be filled by Jesus. Only He can truly satisfy. That is what I had come to understand and to truly believe with all my heart, based on my own personal experience of Him.

I looked again at these dark-eyed Colombian faces and I saw the truth before me. What they possess fills their souls. They have no hunger or thirst, not in terms of the world's understanding, because they are poor people but they are mightily rich in the spiritual sense of the word. They do not have to watch over their possessions to protect them from the thief in the night. They do not have to put their treasures into a bank vault. Their treasures will endure forever and are not subject to decay or inflation. They will neither rust nor wear out. They have been given a cast-iron guarantee, which covers them not only for this life, but also into eternity.

I started to speak, with Reynard at my side translating my words into Spanish. I told them how much it meant to me to be with them and what a privilege it was to come to their church. I said I knew nothing of the kind of persecution that they experienced and so I asked them what would they like me to talk about, what would they like to hear?

The response was quick and certain "Tell us about other persecuted Christians. We want to hear about our brothers who also suffer because of their love for Jesus". I then proceeded to tell them about my trips to China and of one particular wonderful experience of meeting a Chinese brother who helped me take Bibles across a border after I had been apprehended by the authorities. Without his help, I would not have successfully delivered some very much needed Bibles. In helping me he put himself at great risk.

I told my story, hesitating long enough for Reynard to translate. As I spoke, I forgot where I was and I just relived the experience as I have done so many times before. The joy I feel in my heart every time I recall the event is the same as the wonderful joy I felt during the original encounter. I finished my story and looked about me. There were smiles and nods from members of that Colombian congregation.

The Pastor explained to me after the service, that when his flock hear of other brothers and sisters suffering persecution it demonstrates to them that they are not alone, nor are they on their own in their suffering. Others are suffering too in different ways in countries around the world and it gives them courage, strength and perseverance in their own persecution. They then pray for those who suffer with them.

As we said our farewells to the Pastor and the three of us boarded our vehicle to leave, I asked myself again "What am I doing here?" but this time I knew the answer because God had shown me so clearly. There was nothing I could bring to these wonderful Colombian Christians except myself and to follow God's command to go and He would do the rest. I learnt so much that day because he showed that even though I saw myself as small, weak, shy and insignificant, He didn't. The lasting memory will be that, as we arrived at the church and met the Pastor, and again, as we bade him farewell, he said on both occasions and straight from his heart "Thank you so much for coming, it means so much to us. God Bless you for coming to be with us".

"It is so simple." I thought to myself. I had placed little emphasis on, and totally underestimated, the importance of what it meant to these brothers and sisters that we had come to see them, to be with them and to share with them. That is all they wanted from us, as well as our prayers. It was as wonderful and as simple as that.

"COME TO US
AND PRAY FOR US."

A THICK BLACK PLAIT

A thick, black plait of hair hangs down her back. Her dress is thin and worn but is clean, with a fragrance of soap. Her skin is smooth and golden brown. Her eyes seem to fill her face, big brown eyes with long dark lashes. On her feet are worn sandals. She smiles a soft, gentle smile. "What a beautiful child!" I say to myself. For indeed a child is all she is. She has a special glow about her, which has nothing to do with her youth. Her smile comes from her eyes and then lights up her face. Her strong, white teeth are in perfect contrast to her brown, olive skin. She is just fourteen years of age, a young girl, and yet there is something about her that makes you feel she is much older than her years, that you can't quite grasp.

She reminds me of my niece in England. Strange that, because my niece is blonde and fair skinned. Whatever it is that conjures up the image and thoughts of my niece, I do not know. Perhaps it's the smile, yes that's it, it's the smile.

In her arms she cradles a child, about two years of age, a little boy. He clings so tightly to her neck as she rocks him back and forth, a gentle, cradle rock. She looks down at the child now asleep in her arms and I see the look of love in her eyes. His thumb is now in his mouth as he suckles it in sleep. She continues to rock him and snuggles her chin into the soft black curls on the crown of his head. "What a beautiful sight!" I think "A young, loving sister with her baby brother.".

So many times, in this war-ravaged country of Colombia, I have seen too, too many children suffering, who have so little and oh, so many who are orphans. Some are so young they will not be able to remember their parents. When you go to the countless orphanages you feel so helpless. You look into the faces of these children and ask what can you do. The one thing I was told that I could do for them was to put my arms around them and just hold them. All they want is a cuddle, to be held, to feel close to someone, if only for a few moments. As I look at the sleeping boy, I think "How wonderful, at least he has a loving sister to take care of him.".

As I look at her again, I think how marvellous it would have been if I had been blessed with a daughter such as her. She senses me looking at her and breaks off her preoccupation with the small boy. She looks up and smiles at me. She raises her hand and points to the silver crucifix around my neck and says in her broken English "That is beautiful". I touch the cross, a prized possession, given to me out of love from someone so precious to me. I finger the beloved cross. "Yes," I say "it is lovely isn't it?". She nods in assent.

Suddenly we are called to leave, our time in this refugee camp so short. In this country I find that we can, for reasons of safety, only stay for short periods of time. We are constantly on the move.

As I turn to leave this small wooden shack with its hard packed earth floor, I turn to the girl's father, a Pastor who has established a small church in this Colombian refugee camp. I shake his hand. "God bless you Pastor and your work here in this camp. You have been blessed with a lovely daughter and son." He looks quizzically at me and says "She is my daughter, but that child in her arms is not my son. I am his grandfather. That child is her child". "But, Pastor," I say "you told me your daughter was just fourteen years old and that the boy was two years of age". "That is correct", he replies. "But my daughter was raped when she was twelve by a drunken man. That boy is hers." I turn to look back at her and she smiles and says "God bless you and thank you for coming".

I leave the hut with the Pastor and his daughter following behind and make my way to the camp gate. Our driver and our guide, Enrico, are standing by our vehicle.

I turn to say my goodbyes to the Pastor and his daughter, who is cradling the sleeping child in her arms. She smiles a beautiful smile at me. For no apparent reason, I feel my right hand go to the crucifix around my neck and I caress it in my hand. These words, unbidden by me, come into my mind. "Give her the cross". My immediate response is "My cross! But it means so much to me. Oh, not my beautiful cross!". She has seen my gesture. My fingers curl around that lovely silver crucifix but, of course, she is oblivious to the reason for my gesture or the thoughts going through my mind. Her attention is once again fixed upon my cross and she smiles and says "Beautiful!".

Again the words come into my mind. They are clear and firm but spoken with a gentleness. "Give her the cross." Without hesitation, I lift my hands to undo the clasp of the chain which holds it around my neck. Holding the chain by the fingers of each hand, I hold out the cross to her. She doesn't understand, she just continues to smile at me. I then say "This is for you". She turns to her father with a frown on her face. Obviously, not sure whether she has understood what I am saying. I turn to our guide, Enrico, and tell him that I want to give my crucifix to her and ask him to explain that to her. However, for a moment I suddenly think about the implications of my action and how it might rebound on her. I, therefore, ask him whether other refugees in the camp might resent her having such a thing in her possession, believing that if I had met them, then I would be making this gift to them and not to her. My other concern is whether she might get hurt because of having the cross and that someone might steal it from her, or worse, harm or kill her in order to possess it.

I know that I can trust the advice and wisdom of Enrico, a Colombian himself, extremely knowledgeable about refugees and refugee camps. Indeed, he knows the refugees in this camp very well. With complete certainty in his voice, he assures me that no harm will befall her if I give her the cross.

Enrico turns to the girl and, in Spanish, explains to her that the cross is a gift from me to her. His voice takes on a more serious note and I see from the look on her face that she is listening intently to all he is saying. He speaks to her in her native tongue. He seems to be asking and seeking assurances from her that she understands what he is saying and the importance of his words. It is as if he is saying "Accept this gift, but only on the terms and conditions I am giving to you". I watch her face and she solemnly nods in assent. Then Enrico, obviously reassured by the girl, smiles at her and hands the silver crucifix to her. He then speaks briefly to her father, who also nods in assent. It seems to me that an agreement is reached between both men and that her father will ensure that whatever Enrico has said to his daughter will be fulfilled. The young girl lifts up the cross and as it dangles from its chain, it gently sways. The rays of the sun catch it and the cross sparkles and dances in the sunlight, a truly delightful and wonderful sight to behold.

With her face full of joy, she gives the cross back to me and then, turning around, she lifts up her lovely thick, black plait so that I can put the cross around her neck. I fasten the clasp and she says in her broken English "Oh, thank you. Thank you and God bless you".

We turn and wave before getting into our vehicle and as we drive away, the Pastor and his daughter continue to wave until we are out of sight. I lean forward in my seat and speak to Enrico and ask him what he had said to the young girl before she accepted the crucifix. He says that he had told her that she was not in any way to look upon it as an icon or something to be worshipped as an object in itself. The cross was a reminder of what the Lord had done for her and for all of mankind. He had died on the cross that she might live. It was a symbol of the Lord's unshakeable love for her. Her father had said that he would ensure that his daughter always viewed the cross around her neck in that way.

As our vehicle travels along the dusty road, I reflect on the events of the morning and my hand goes to my throat, but my all too familiar cross is no longer there. I have to ask myself a question and I have to be completely honest with myself. I need to be sure that my act had not just been an emotional, knee jerk response to the specific circumstances surrounding me in that refugee camp, a gesture based on pity or sorrow or the need to respond in some way so that I felt that I had done something, whatever that something might be. I know that before I move forward and into the rest of the day and the days to follow, that I have to clear this issue in my mind once and for all, so that there would be no room in the future for any lingering regrets about the loss of my crucifix.

But it isn't what I am thinking, it is what I am feeling. Within my heart there is an absolute one hundred per cent certainty that there would never be any regrets. I know that what I had done, what had taken place, was exactly what the Lord had intended. That cross was not for me to keep. It had been loaned to me for a while until I came to this place in order to give it to this young Colombian girl. I am then reminded of the words that Enrico had uttered to her before she accepted the cross. The cross is a reminder of what the Lord has done for us, it is not an object in its own right to be worshipped as some kind of holy relic. These words, I realise, were meant just as much for me as they were for her. "That's right." I think. "We should always focus on Jesus and not be distracted by objects and symbols. He is all that matters and we carry Him in our hearts wherever we go or whatever we might do".

I bless that young Colombian girl and her child. In my mind's eye I see again her lovely smiling face and that thick, black plait hanging down her back and I murmer, "God bless you child".

A CARGO OF LOVE

Heads bent low, eyes glancing from under shielded eyelids, darting, furtive, full of fear. Noise, car horns, raised high-pitched voices, police whistles blowing, noise of car engines, a babble of voices, rushing people, frantic scurrying. Bicycles, hundreds of them, cyclists riding so close to each other, riding in front of each other, missing cars by a hair's breadth. The dust, the noise, the polluted air. No silence, no peace, a mass of humanity in fear. This is the China I saw. Faces old and worn before their time. Weary, careworn, no joy, no laughter, too much to do and too much to think about. There is no peace, no harmony in this city of Babel.

We move at a gentle pace, our destination known. We push through the crowds, making steady progress with the noise and the cacophony of sound ringing in our ears. The back-pack is heavy and the luggage we pull is square in shape and hard to the touch. People rush past us, no time for them to smile. We are just a few westerners with lots of luggage, not an unusual sight in this country.

As we walk along hot dusty streets, it seems as if the whole population is on the move. The flow of humanity is coming towards us and it's as if we are going against the tide. They are going in one direction to fulfil their purpose and we are going in the opposite direction to fulfil a God-given purpose.

We pray silently as we walk, we pray for the safety of the brothers we are seeking to meet. We do not know their names, not their real names and we do not speak their language. We only know that the cargo we carry on our backs and pull behind us will satisfy a desperate need. Indeed, these people are desperate people. Their need is greater than any addiction known to man, whether it be the love of an alcoholic for his bottle, a drug addict for his needle, or the gambler waiting for that vital turn of the card that will secure him the game of all games that will give him that ultimate prize. Their addiction leads them not only to prison and torture but also to face death. If they do survive, then once released from custody, they are under surveillance, their movements carefully monitored by the security police.

They can never be "free" again and if one night that brother is found dead in a dark alley, murdered, assailant unknown, how many people will care? If someone is brave enough to ask questions of the authorities, they will be met with a shrug of the shoulders, just another person who has decided that life is no longer worth living and believes that their only option is for them to end their life. It happens a lot, the authorities say, and with a population of 1.2 billion, who will worry if one solitary Chinese life has been snuffed out? After all, there are millions more to take their place. So, with an addiction so strong that men and women will lay down their lives, how can you not respond to their need and not take to them their heart's desire?

The precious cargo we carry is with us for only a short time. We release that cargo of love and eternity into the hands of those we will never see again, at least not this side of heaven. The handover of the Bibles takes place. In what is a fleeting moment they are gone. No more than a quick handshake, a whispered blessing "God bless you, brother". Momentarily, there is a glance into dark, loving eyes, crowned beneath black eyebrows and jet black hair. A smile for you which says it all. No need for words, language is not needed. The expression on their faces is enough, for they reflect the joy of the Lord from within them. The Holy Spirit within you leaps in response to the Holy Spirit within them. They turn and are soon gone, back into the crowd. The dark heads are now lost amongst those of their own people. We watch after them for a few moments, then we turn and empty-handed we walk away.

For me, at that moment, a thousand questions flood my mind. Where will that precious cargo go? How far north, south, east or west will it travel? Will the Bibles go to villages, towns or cities and how many underground churches will receive copies? What will the reaction be of brothers and sisters who have never before held such a precious gift of a Chinese Bible in their hands? Will there be tears, smiles, great joy? I guess so. Will one heavenly gift be taken, a page carefully torn out and given to one brother or sister, who will copy, copy and copy it again to make more precious gifts for other brothers and sisters? Who knows where that holy cargo will go? Only our heavenly Father.

Thinking again of those care-worn faces, so full of worry, which we passed on our journey, I pray for them and I pray that they will receive the very precious gift of one of these Bibles. I pray that their tears will be turned to laughter, their fears to joy and for a peace and contentment to rest within them so that their faces reflect the love of God in their lives.

We return from whence we came and tomorrow another precious cargo of love will be entrusted into our care, for us to take across another border to another unknown brother.

I then ask myself what greater privilege can there be, than to carry our Lord's precious gift of love and eternal life to his beloved children of China. Once again, I thank God for this wonderful privilege.

THE END

TAKE TIME TO PAUSE AND THINK

As Christians living in the West, we can easily be lulled into the trap of relying on our material comforts, rather than on our Lord for our security. One of the effects of this is that we take too much for granted. Our needs and expectations of life are high and we become ungrateful and even stressed when things do not go our way.

Those who have had the privilege of meeting Christians living in poverty and under great pressure so often find that, in contrast, they are joyful and thankful in all circumstances. So, when we become involved with our suffering brothers, we not only help them with our prayers and other support but we also have much to learn from them for our own Christian walk.

In addition, if we do not obey the Biblical commands to help those "members of the body" that are suffering, we may feel the effects here in our country. Not only will our weakness and complacency encourage the persecutors to think that they can mistreat our brethren, but that same complacency will encourage those who wish to suppress Christianity at home to do the same here. Perhaps this is already beginning to be the case!!!

So, as we obey the Scriptures in Proverbs 31:8 and Hebrews 13:3, and intercede in both prayer and action for the persecuted Church, let us pray that our obedience will help to protect us from similar persecution.

HOW YOU CAN HELP

Throughout the world our brothers meet secretly in forests, on deserted beaches, by riverbanks, in basements, attics and other such places in order to glorify the name of our beloved Lord. There are thousands upon thousands of Christian brothers who are suffering and dying in dozens of captive nations, as well as those brothers who now lie in countless, nameless graves, who died for their faith.

> *"Do not abandon us.*
> *Do not forget us.*
> *Continue to pray for us.*
> *Come and meet with us.*
> *Give us the tools we need*
> *and we will willingly pay the price for using them.*
> *Give us Bibles."*

Hear, then, the cries of your brothers in captive nations. They do not ask for escape, safety or an easy life. They ask for Bibles to use in spreading the Word of God. How can they spread the Word of God if they do not possess it?

Western Christians can help in a tremendous way by praying for our persecuted brothers, as well as praying for their persecutors that they may be saved.

You and your church can help by donating money to purchase Bibles to be sent to persecuted Christians. Thousands and thousands of Christians have never seen a Bible but, so desperate are they to hold a Bible in their hands, they willingly face great danger and even death in order to possess one.

In so many countries throughout the world the drama, bravery and martyrdom of the Early Church is happening all over again and the free church in the western world sleeps. Our brothers, alone and without help, are waging the greatest, most courageous battle of this century, equal to the heroism, courage and dedication of the Early Church. And the church sleeps on, oblivious of their struggle and agony, just as Peter, James and John slept in the moment of their Saviour's agony in the Garden of Gethsemane.

Ask yourself "Will you sleep whilst your brothers in Christ suffer and fight for the Gospel?" Please help them now. There are so many things you can do:

1) PRAY FOR THEM (set up a prayer group)

2) WRITE TO THEM

3) PROVIDE FUNDS IN ORDER TO PURCHASE BIBLES FOR THEM

4) TAKE BIBLES TO OUR BROTHERS

OPEN DOORS

OPEN DOORS is an organisation that has been serving persecuted Christians worldwide for many years. They define their ministry as follows:

1. To strengthen the body of Christ living under restriction or persecution by providing and delivering Bibles, training and other support materials.

2. To train and encourage the body of Christ in threatened or unstable areas, to prepare believers to face persecution and suffering and equip them to maintain a witness to the gospel of Christ.

3. To motivate, mobilise and educate the church in the free world to identify with and become more involved in assisting the suffering church, believing that when "One member suffers, all the members suffer with it" (Corinthians 12:26, New King James Version)

IF YOU WANT FURTHER INFORMATION ON HOW YOU OR YOUR CHURCH CAN HELP, OR IF YOU WOULD LIKE AN OPEN DOORS REPRESENTATIVE TO COME AND SHARE WITH YOUR CHURCH OR CHURCH GROUP THEN PLEASE WRITE TO:

Open Doors UK
PO Box 6
Witney
Oxon
OX 29 6WG

Like Esther, I too have taken Bibles to 'closed countries'. Esther asked if I would tell you my story of how I became one of God's travellers.

TREVOR'S STORY

I had been aware of the plight of my brothers and sisters across the world, who are suffering for their faith, for quite a while. I did my best to support them when I could - from the comfort of England. A member of the leadership team of my church made regular trips into "closed countries" and had suggested, on more than one occasion, that I join him.

I felt that I would like to go, but I wasn't sure that my faith would be strong enough. It would be just me and God out there and anything could happen - could I trust Him? There was only one way to find out.

It was while I was pondering on this that, one summer evening, I went to a meeting in a tent, which was part of a Bible week being held at Calver in the beautiful Derbyshire countryside. The inspirational preacher was speaking about how often people sit in church or meetings like this one, thinking and talking about going out to serve God and preparing to go for 20 years or so, but they never actually go.

This made me think about my reason for not going when the opportunity had arisen. I reasoned that my family were my priority at the time. They needed me and I had to ensure that there was enough money to see my two teenage sons through college and university. Then, I got to thinking that this might just be an excuse. After all, my father had recently died and he had left me some money, which, if I was honest, would be enough to cover the cost of the boys' education.

So, there I was without an excuse! I wondered if God was speaking to me about this and so I asked him for a sign and just at this point we started to sing the hymn "I the Lord of Sea and Sky". I had never heard this before, but the words, especially of the chorus, had a dramatic effect on me.

> *"Here I am, Lord,*
> *Is it I, Lord?*
> *I have heard you calling in the night.*
> *I will go, Lord*
> *If you lead me,*
> *I will hold your people in my heart.*[1]*"*

It did, indeed, seem that God could be speaking personally to me here.

I said "Not bad, Lord." But, like Gideon, I said to God "I want to turn the fleece and I want it to be dry this time. Give me another sign." [2]

Instantly, into my head came the words "Luke 10:19". I had no idea what this scripture could be, so grabbing my Bible, I looked it up there and then. This is what I read:

"Behold, I give you the authority to trample on serpents and scorpions, over all the power of the enemy; and nothing shall by any means hurt you." (New King James translation of the Bible)

This inspired me. I knew I could trust God to get me there and bring me back safely and to look after my family while I was away. So, as soon as the meeting ended, I walked round the tent to the brother from church who had been asking me to travel with him and said "Where are we going?". My first trip was to China and then to Vietnam the following January.

I tested God on this and subsequent trips and found Him to be faithful and true to His word. I encourage you to do the same.

Trevor
Bible Traveller

---

[1] The hymn containing the chorus "Here I am, Lord" can be found on page 96.

[2] See Chapter 6 of the Book of Judges for the story of Gideon.

QUOTE

"Those who have had the privilege of meeting Christians living under oppression and under great pressure so often find that, in contrast, they are joyful and thankful in all circumstances. So, when we become involved with our suffering brothers, we not only help them with our prayers and other support, but we also have much to learn from them for our own Christian walk."

A Bible Traveller

Thank you dear reader for allowing me to share just some of my experiences and those of my brothers with you.

God bless you in abundance.

Esther Davenport

I, THE LORD OF SEA AND SKY

I, the Lord of sea and sky,
I have heard my people cry.
All who dwell in dark or sin, my hand will save.
I, who made the stars of night,
I will make their darkness bright.
Who will bear my light to them?
Who shall I send?

(CHORUS) *Here I am, Lord,*
Is it I, Lord?
I have heard you calling in the night.
I will go, Lord,
If You lead me,
I will hold Your people in my heart.

I, the Lord of snow and rain,
I have borne my people's pain.
I have wept for love of them.
They turn away.
I will break their hearts of stone,
Give them hearts for love alone.
I will speak my words to them.
Who shall I send?

(CHORUS)

I, the Lord of wind and flame,
I will tend the poor and lame.
I will set a feast for them.
My hand will save.
Finest bread I will provide,
Till their hearts be satisfied.
I will give my life to them.
Who shall I send?

(CHORUS)